What is a Social Movement?

What is Sociology?

What is a Social Movement?

HANK JOHNSTON

polity

First published in 2014 by Polity Press

Polity Press
65 Bridge Street
Cambridge CB2 1UR, UK

Polity Press
350 Main Street
Malden, MA 02148, USA

ISBN-13: 978-0-7456-6084-4
ISBN-13: 978-0-7456-6085-1(pb)

A catalog record for this book is available from the British Library.

Typeset in 10.5 on 12 pt Sabon
by Toppan Best-set Premedia Limited
Printed and bound in Great Britain by T.J. International, Padstow, Cornwall

The publisher has used its best endeavors to ensure that the URLs for external websites referred to in this book are correct and active at the time of going to press. However, the publisher has no responsibility for the websites and can make no guarantee that a site will remain live or that the content is or will remain appropriate.

Every effort has been made to trace all copyright holders, but if any have been inadvertently overlooked the publisher will be pleased to include any necessary credits in any subsequent reprint or edition.

For further information on Polity, visit our website: www.politybooks.com

Contents

1

What is a Social Movement?

Social movements are key forces of social change in the modern world. Although not all social change emanates from them – technological innovation, climate change, natural disasters, and wars also are causes – social movements are unique because they are guided purposively and strategically by the people who join them. Another key characteristic is that they mobilize and do their business mostly outside established political and institutional channels. This makes questions of their origin and growth especially compelling for the social scientist. Some social movements represent efforts by citizens to collectively create a more just and equitable world. Other movements are motivated by compelling grievances that push their adherents out of their ordinary daily routines. Social movements are typically resisted by forces that favor the status quo, which imparts a fundamental contentiousness to movement actions. But the defining characteristic of all movements, big and small, is that they move history along, sometimes in significant ways. Knowing what they are and how social scientists study them are important tasks if we are to understand contemporary society and where it is headed.

In 2011, *Time* magazine selected "the protester" as its person of the year. This was partly because movements in opposition to repressive regimes exploded that year in North Africa and the Middle East. In both Egypt and Tunisia, the Mubarak and the Ben-Ali regimes were brought down by unexpected mass movements of political opposition. In Syria, a similar opposition movement took a different course. It spiraled into a civil war with casualties over 100,000 and a flow of refugees approaching 1.5 million. Many social movements voice wide-ranging demands for political change – in these cases, demands for the overthrow of the old regime and the ushering in of a new, more democratic system.

Also that year, another wave of protests occurred in several Western countries in the form of the Occupy movement in the US, the 15-M (for May 15) movement in Spain, and large anti-austerity protests in the UK, Ireland, and Greece. These protests shared common themes that grew out of the global economic collapse, the complicity of political elites, and their failures regarding economic policy. These movements were less successful in achieving their immediate goals, but they did create networks of activists, linked by the new social media, which serve as the basis for continued social-change activism. They also elaborated new tactics of site occupations of central squares and plazas and radical participatory democracy that will have strategic effects in other future movements.

In addition, a huge but less bounded cultural shift is occurring in North America and Europe, again precipitated by a social movement. I have in mind the gay rights movement, a network of organizations and groups that are less in the headlines than the above two examples, but which have worked for decades to fight discrimination, promote equality, and change attitudes about homosexuality and marriage. In the US just twenty years earlier, the Defense of Marriage Act, which banned gay marriage at the federal level, was passed by the Clinton administration with little congressional opposition. Today, a majority of US citizens are not opposed to gay marriage. Ex-President Clinton (and his wife – perhaps a future president) both publicly affirm that the Defense of Marriage Act was a mistake. While gay marriage still remains a contentious issue, it is fair to say that this shift in public opinion would not have occurred without the various campaigns of the gay rights movement.

These are different kinds of movements. Those that occurred as part of the Arab Spring were obviously political, and protesters risked a great deal taking action against repressive states. In democratic polities such as Spain and the United States, social movements are quite common, and at any given time the analyst finds numerous movements mobilizing on a wide variety of issues and claims. They are an important part of the political landscape whereby diverse groups and organizations promote their interests, make demands, and articulate their visions of change. The gay rights movement has political dimensions as it fights for marriage equality, which means that it must fight against legislation such as the Defense of Marriage Act and against the anti-gay marriage Proposition 8 in my home state of California. But it also has a cultural dimension in changing ideas about marriage, sexuality, and gendered performances that may be less apparent but no less important in the scope of social change. Numerous groups and organizations in the GLBT (for gay, lesbian, bisexual, and transgender) movement have contributed to this effort over the years in different ways.

It is a large undertaking to navigate the complexity of these political, cultural, and organizational elements in a research project, and the analyst must make decisions about where to begin, which groups to include and which not to, what to focus on and what to place aside. Moreover, every social researcher knows how essential it is to define one's terms precisely. A good starting place for this book is to clarify those decisions about how we come to know about a social movement – its boundaries regarding which groups, ideas, and actions are included and which ones are not.

The Study of Social Movements

I approach the study of social movements guided by Charles Tilly's observation (1978: 8–9) that the field's basic analytical dimensions are: (1) the groups and organizations that make up a collective action; (2) the events that are part of the action repertoire; and (3) the ideas that unify the groups and guide their protests. He stressed that, when we study social movements, we tend to focus on just one of this trinity, which, in turn, pulls us into related areas of the other two spheres.

For example, if we are interested in studying a protest event – say, a huge antiwar protest in a large city – we are invariably drawn to the groups that organized it and then their ideas, which motivated their actions. Much has changed in the field of social movement research since Tilly offered these ideas, and they can be fine-tuned to better reflect how the field has advanced, while still maintaining the insight that a focus on one draws the analyst to the relevance of the others.

First, a large body of research has emerged to show that movement groups and organizations do not stand alone but rather are linked in network structures through overlapping memberships, interrelations among members, and contacts among leaders (Diani 1992; Diani and McAdam 2003; della Porta and Diani 2006). Taking into account the network structure of a movement that ties together various organizations of different size and formality, it is more accurate to refer to the broader *structural sphere* of a movement. It is a label that captures the relatively fixed networked relations among groups, organizations and individual participants that characterize social movements large and small. The structural sphere is a crucial focus because it is through interlinkages among organizations that resources are brought to bear for mobilization – getting people into the streets and applying pressure on politicians. These ties are also the skeletal structure of a movement's unity and continuity. Groups can dissolve and organizations can be torn by schisms, but the general movement is characterized by temporal persistence beyond the fate of just one group.

Second, the ideas that fuel a movement, guide it, and give it cohesion include the time-tested and widely studied notions of ideologies, goals, values, and interests. In recent years, however, researchers have probed the concept of collective identity as a key ideational element that binds together the individuals and groups within a movement. Also, an important theoretical insight that has been widely applied in movement research is the concept of collective action frames. These are cognitive schemata that guide interpretation of events for movement participants, bystander publics, and political elites, and are distinct from a systematic ideology or vaguely defined cultural values and norms. Research has emphasized that both collective identity and interpretative frames are ongoing collective elaborations anchored in situations of interaction. This is a finding that moves research on these ideational dimensions from books, ideological tracts, and manifestos where movement goals and demands are expressed, to spoken interactions among participants. Thus I will use the term *ideational–interpretative sphere* of a social movement to capture how the analytical scope of a movement's ideas have been broadened in recent years.

Third, I extend Tilly's focus on the events to include all the elements in a movement's repertoire, how they are performed, and how they are reacted to. Tilly had been instrumental in developing a performative approach to social movements based on his concept of the modern social movement repertoire (1995, 2005, 2008). An emphasis on the *performances* of a movement rather than its protest events also follows cultural sociology's basic insight of social action as theatre. I emphasize the performance metaphor because, just as in other forms of social behavior, typical movement performances – street protests, demonstrations, strikes, marches, and so on – are strongly symbolic in the sense that they are making statements beyond just the content of their songs, chants, placards, and speeches. Also, they are performances because they always have an audience: those who witness the performances, interpret what they see, act upon their interpretations, and whose presence influences how the performance unfolds. Viewing a social movement protest as a performance puts it in its full context of the actors and the various audiences, and broadens the way we study social movements by situating them in dynamic relationships.

Figure 1.1 graphically represents a general model of how social scientists approach the study of social movements. The circles represent the three analytical spheres broadly: social structure, cultural ideations/interpretations, and the social performances of daily life. The core of the figure depicts the convergence of those elements characteristic of social movements. Putting it simply, the core concentrates (1) those interlinked groups and organizations that (2) carry and expound ideational–interpretative elements, such as identities, ideologies, and frames, that are (3) reflected and manifested in collective performances that we recognize as part of the modern social movement repertoire. The core region is where

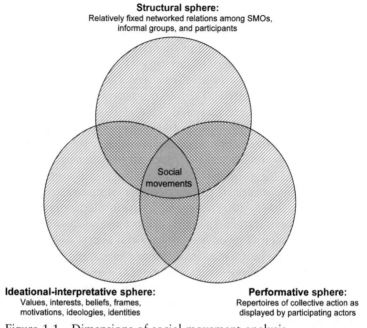

Figure 1.1   Dimensions of social movement analysis

the analyst of social movements concentrates attention. Although one's interest originally may be focused on just one of the three spheres – a particular group's ideology, for example – the researcher is invariably drawn to other groups (via network ties) which share similar ideas, and how they translate their ideas to action. Implied is that there is an iterative and reinforcing relationship among the three. The figure also portrays three crosshatched areas that bud out from its core where only two spheres intersect. These areas capture how related groups, ideas, and actions that are not strictly part of the movement still may be interesting to the researcher because they occupy a middle ground that is less removed from ordinary, instutionalized social relations but at the same time supportive of social change. For example, a variety of groups – NGOs (nongovernmental organizations), advocacy organizations, and interest groups, all of which I will discuss shortly – would fall into this category and be located in the upper left of the three secondary areas.

Each of the larger spheres represents a fundamental dimension of social life with a wide distribution of different forms and foci, but the social movement analyst is interested in those that congeal towards center by virtue of how they challenge the status quo through extraordinary, noninstitutional actions. Let us take a closer look at the elements that concentrate at the core and how they give definition to what a social movement is.

The Structure of Social Movements

In the study of social movements, there are two basic ways of thinking about the structural sphere – that is, the relatively fixed and enduring relations among the social actors. First, social movements are composed of groups and organizations, large and small, contentious and tamed, that integrate individual members in varying degrees of participation and mobilize them to action. It is fair to say that these are basic units of movement structure, but – as I mentioned – there are also related groups that are relevant: advocacy groups, interest groups, and NGOs, and we need to differentiate among them as foci of study. Second, social movements are *network structures*. Given the ideological, tactical, and organizational complexity of social movements, a network organization interconnects this complexity, binding the components together, and imparting an overall cohesion. Just as some movement participants have multiple memberships, some organizations draw more members and have more central positions in the interconnected movement network.

Social movement organizations

A common error among beginning students is to mistake the organizations of a movement for the movement itself. In the case of the environmental movement, Greenpeace, Friends of the Earth, or the Earth Liberation Front are *social movement organizations*, or simply SMOs. These are groups varying in their size, complexity, and formal structure that are organized by citizens to pursue their claims when politicians are unresponsive or when certain issues seem especially compelling. Sometimes SMOs are highly formalized and grow quite large, commanding vast resources, like Greenpeace or Nature Conservancy. But studying just the large SMOs would miss the breadth and complexity of the environmental movement. In addition to the large and significant SMO players, social movements also include small groups, some quite informal, that may be dedicated to somewhat different goals, but are, overall, guided by an environmentalist ethos. For example, groups of friends and acquaintances might create gardens in urban spaces, or encourage the use of bicycles instead of gas-guzzling cars and trucks. Social movements, in general, are complicated aggregations of diverse groups and individuals. The structural and organizational bases of social movements, taken as a whole, are usually diverse and complex, and always interrelated in a network of connections among different SMOs, informal groups, bystanders not yet fully committed to the movement, and individuals who may be favorably disposed to the movement but have not yet acted.

The centrality of SMOs in the study of social movements was first emphasized by John McCarthy and Mayer Zald (1973, 1977). They observed that a trend in modern movements was that SMOs were becoming larger, more formalized, and professionalized. They used the term *professional social movement organization* to refer to the increasing complexity of SMOs, often meaning full-time, salaried staffs. It should not be surprising, then, that some of the major figures in the field of study are also specialists in the analysis of complex organizations. The trend to professionalization contrasts with *grassroots organizations* that may arise more spontaneously and informally from an aggrieved population. Large change-oriented organizations may increase efficiency in planning and fundraising, thereby bringing in greater resources to be put at the disposal of movement goals, but they also have a downside in limiting member input and democratic decision making. Also, Piven and Cloward's classic study (1977) showed that large organizations were less likely to wage disruptive campaigns, which are the most effective tactics for resource-poor groups. Although professional SMOs tend to tame a movement's tactical repertoire, the overall trend is that they wield more and more influence in social movements, which means they are in positions to draw even more resources and influence, and grow and professionalize even more. This is a process that tends to marginalize smaller groups that comprise the movement.

Among the largest SMOs, marketing has become a big part of the professionalization trend. I regularly get glossy direct-mail solicitations from the Sierra Club, Amnesty International, Nature Conservancy, and other mega-SMOs. These mailings are costly to produce and require the purchase of mailing lists from other organizations, which is how I got on their lists – thanks to my wife who joined the Sierra Club a few years ago. Fundraising creates its own internal dynamic because of the high costs of direct mail and canvassing campaigns. They require a staff to design and direct them, which is a diversion of staff from the change-oriented goals of the movement. These large SMOs are more bureaucratically organized in that staff members have clear areas of authority and responsibility, of which direct-mail marketing is one.

Another trend is that the largest ones are becoming transnational in scope. These are sometimes huge organizations, such as Greenpeace and Friends of the Earth International. Transnational SMOs (TSMOs) will vary in their degree of centralization and coordination. Friends of the Earth is a decentralized organization, but other professionalized SMOs are more bureaucratic and hierarchical, such as Greenpeace, Worldwide Fund for Wildlife, Oxfam, or Amnesty International. These SMOs have main offices in Washington DC or London, and branches in other cities of the world. The paid staffs are professionals who must be educated, socially and linguistically skilled, and technically conversant in their areas of activism. Lahusen (2005) has traced the "cocktail circuit" of staff members of transnational environmental and human rights groups in Brussels and Geneva as they seek to influence the policymakers there.

The line separating large SMOs from *interest groups* that pursue more institutional approaches to political influence is often blurred. Interest groups are key sources of political influence in contemporary Western democracies. They are close cousins to SMOs because they apply pressure to politicians and exist on the fringes of established party politics, but are not so far removed from established activities that they would be called extrainstitutional in the same way that SMOs are. Interest groups are everywhere in modern democracies (Knoke 1986; Clemens 1997). Labor unions, ethnic-cultural groups such as the National Association for the Advancement of Colored People (NAACP) and Mexican-American Legal Defense and Educational Fund, and industry groups like the National Association of Manufacturers, US Chamber of Commerce, and National Mining Association are just a few examples of large, formal, and complex organizations that represent the interests of economic and social groups. In the never-ending debate about guns and assault weapons in the US, the National Rifle Association is an interest group that wields great power and influence.

Terms like *nongovernmental organizations* and *advocacy organizations* are often applied to formal groups that pursue value-based, change-oriented goals on specific issues such as human rights, peace issues, land mines, or human trafficking. Amnesty International (AI) is a huge international organization that pursues multipronged initiatives on human rights, such as advocating for political prisoners, publicizing persecution of oppositional activists, and monitoring torture and disappearances of political activists. But if the analyst steps back to frame the "human rights movement," then AI certainly occupies a prominent place there as a highly professionalized and effective SMO (or TSMO, for its transnational scope). But it is also an international nongovernmental organization (INGO), or, from another perspective, might be seen as part of a transnational advocacy network (TAN) for human rights. This alphabet soup of terms reminds us of the fundamental observation that much depends on how the analyst chooses to approach the phenomenon being studied. None of the labels are incorrect, strictly speaking, and can be said to reflect the starting point taken by the analyst in figure 1.1.

Social movement networks

Researchers have long recognized that social networks play key roles in recruitment, organization, and coordination processes of social movements (Gerlach and Hine 1970; Diani 1992; Diani and McAdam 2003; della Porta and Diani 2006). Here, I stress that the skeletal support of a network structure imparts integrity and loose unity to the swirling and buzzing confusion of the organizational and ideological complexity in large movements. Networks are relatively permanent, but allow for flexible coordination among individuals and groups that, otherwise, go about their own business and pursue their specific movement-related goals. Through informal contacts, semiformal overlapping memberships, and formalized interlinkages characteristic of some global organizations, such as the Rainforest Action Network or the Peoples' Global Action, networks allow for the autonomy of local member groups while providing the basis for information exchange and coordination. It is common that campaigns involving several movement groups are organized on the basis of temporary networks. A social movement can be characterized by the density and number of the connections that make it up. These can be strong or weak, and can vary in their centralization in several key individuals, groups, or organizations. Not only are individuals embedded in networks, but groups and organizations can be analyzed by number and quality of their connections as well.

Figure 1.2 shows the network, not of individuals, but of organizations that made up the environmental movement in

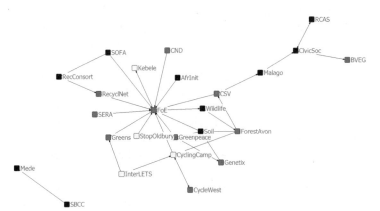

Figure 1.2   Network of environmental SMOs in Bristol, UK
Source: Diani 2011

the city of Bristol, UK, in the early 2000s. Several organizations are interlinked, measured by either reports of contacts or interlinked memberships. The local Friends of the Earth (FoE) group appears to be very central to the network, which suggests that its members would be influential in other groups. Some of the groups are outliers, weakly connected, and in the lower left-hand of the network, one finds two connected groups, but each without ties to others. And this is in only one city. Ponder for a moment the complexity of network ties among environmental SMOs in other cities and towns, and the interconnections that exist among different localities, and you will get a sense of the expanse and interconnectedness inherent in social movement networks – in this case, the environmental movement in the UK.

Movements of Ideas

I take the position in this book that *social movements are characterized by big, change-oriented ideas* that guide them and impart to them an overall unity. In what we might consider to be the grandest movements of all, namely, the great social revolutions of history, the goals are huge, aimed at changing the very social, political, and economic organization of society, and the ideologies are vast, proposing new ways of thinking about human relations and human nature: for example the French Revolution, the Russian Revolution, the Iranian Revolution. The study of revolutions has a long tradition in sociology and political science, and there is a synergy between the development of revolutionary situations and social movement mobilization. Although most social movements are a step or two down the ladder regarding their scope of change, let me be clear: I am defining social movements as big-idea trends, such as environmentalism, feminism, racial equality, gender equality – the sweeping ideas of contemporary history. Movements of the past were about similarly sweeping ideas, such as giving Catholics the vote in nineteenth-century Britain or women the vote in the twentieth-century United States.

Researchers also study many movements that are further down the ladder, for example those focused on specific policy issues, such as the Townsend movement's call for old-age pensions in the United States (Amenta and Zylan 1991), or the movement against nuclear energy (Gamson 1989, 1992a). These are big ideas too, but just slightly less sweeping in their visions of the future. They are characteristic of numerous "smaller" social movements, and it is fair to say that the sweep of the discipline in recent years, as judged by the research topics appearing in the field's major journal, *Mobilization*, has been largely to focus on these kinds of movements. However, this big-versus-small-idea distinction means that, in choosing a research focus, the student of social movements must be sensitive to how far down the ladder one can go and still lay claim to the label "social movement" instead of more bounded concepts such as "protest campaigns," "challenging groups," or "protest events." Let us try to sort through some of these lexical choices.

Near my university, landlords were buying old houses and dividing them up into "minidorms" to house four or five, sometimes more, students. This caused increased traffic congestion and parking problems, not to mention disturbing-the-peace complaints on weekends. Neighbors organized a group to fight this trend via the city council, calling for a resolution to block further division of neighborhood homes. This is a smaller and more informal sort of grassroots collective action, sometimes called a *NIMBY movement* – for "Not In My Back Yard." Its focused demands contrast with the broad trends of social change embodied in environmentalism or feminism, for example. The "NIMBY movement" label, in fact, is unfortunate because what we have here is not a movement in the strictest sense, but one group – a rather small one at that – pursuing its concrete interests. Most NIMBYs fall short on the expansiveness of their *ideations* regarding social change. *Ideology*, in terms of a systematic and internally consistent body of thought, would not even be an appropriate term here. Most also fall short on the structural dimension: in this case, there is just one group. Finally, they fall short regarding their performance repertoire, which, in the present case, was aimed at pressuring the city council through letter-writing and attendance at council meetings. The group, Allied Gardens Citizens against Minidorms, as it was called, was an *interest group* or a *challenging group* – depending on the analyst's preference – but not an expansive social movement. While there was an extrainstitutional quality in its formation, and while it is clearly a case of collective action, definitionally, it does not cross the "social movement" threshold.

This does not imply that the study of NIMBYs cannot make contributions to the field. Movements that are higher up the ladder in terms of scope of change typically include a diversity of challenging groups, sometimes ones that are quite small. Understanding the processes that lead to successful collective action within a single group can be generalizable to other settings. Also, groups that are focused on specific interests can branch out and form networks with similar groups elsewhere. I have in mind citizens' initiatives against big-box superstores such as Wal-Mart, Costco, and Sam's Club (Halebsky 2006). Neighborhood claims against these stores have parallels with the minidorm initiative in San Diego – such as increased traffic, decreasing property values, diminished neighborhood cohesion, and quality of life issues among residents. The difference is that campaigns against big-box stores occur in many communities in North America and the UK. In the US, a growing network among these initiatives has developed, to exchange information and compare strategic initiatives, imparting a more expansive organization on the structural dimension of the phenomenon.

On the ideological–interpretative dimension, this facilitates the development of a fundamental critique against these huge retailers, which – although varying in its elaboration among different groups – nevertheless shifts the configuration of goals, objectives, and rationales a notch upward beyond raw self-serving interest. The ideological critique goes something like this: the expansive plans of these large chain-stores reflect how big, private investment capital assaults the quality of life in old, sometimes poor, neighborhoods in the relentless search of profits. This reframes the threat from an obvious interest-based claim typical of most NIMBYs into a broader interpretation. Participants also embrace tactics from the social movement repertoire, such as demonstrating outside other stores and petitioning, in addition to more institutional approaches such as writing to city council members and planning authorities. These anti-superstore mobilizations may not have the scope of environmentalism or feminism, nor challenge established cultural and institutional patterns in the same way that the GLBT movement does, but on a smaller scale, if the analyst steps back to see its broader dimensions, one can make a case for the social movement label in terms of its networked structure, its broad ideational–interpretative critique, and its performances within the modern movement repertoire.

Ideas that envision new social arrangements, new possibilities, new policies, and new political alignments give social movements shape and motion. The ideational–interpretative dimension includes ideologies, interests, goals, collective identities, values, beliefs, attitudes, frames of interpretation, and norms of behavior, including shared action repertoires such as specific tactics, songs, slogans, and so on. Of all these, four stand out as central in defining a social movement and, therefore, as foci in studying them: ideologies, collective action frames, collective interests, and collective identities. These are the major elements of a social movement's ideational–interpretative dimension and traditionally have been considered key components of its culture.

Ideologies

A fundamental concept in the analysis of movements is *ideology*. Ideologies focus on ideas, on their systematic relation to each other, and on their implications for social and political action based on value commitments. Ideologies specify a movement's goals, what they aspire to. A simple definition would be that an ideology is "a system of ideas that couples assertions and theories about the nature of social life with values and norms relevant to goals that promote or resist social change" (Oliver and Johnston 2005: 192). In this definition, the reference to values highlights the moral and ethical elements of ideologies, while the normative emphasis refers to standards of behavior, especially those behaviors that are guided by goals of social change and that work to foster a sense of common identity among members. Also, ideologies often make assertions about how society works and about human nature. Analysts also point out that ideologies, although they make moral claims, are also reflections of collective interests. For example, neoliberal ideology makes moral claims about the economic benefits of free global trade, but a common criticism is that the benefits mostly accrue to economic elites. Conversely, the ideology of democratic socialism challenges the privileges of economic and political elites in favor of the working classes and middle classes.

Some ideologies are complex, comprehensive, and elaborately codified, as was Marxism–Leninism for the Bolsheviks in the Russian Revolution, or Maoism during the Chinese Revolution, or, from a contemporary perspective, fundamentalist, Salifist Islam. Other ideologies are loosely agreed upon, and, as a result, disagreed upon from time to time, offering participants room for differing interpretations. Examples here would be the varieties of anarchism among some groups that participate in anti-neoliberalism protests, or the convergence of ideas about equality, rights, and gender difference among different sectors of the gay and lesbian movement. These ideologies and the interrelated ideas they embrace are the glue that helps bind people together into the groups, organizations, and networks of the structural sphere. Highly codified ideologies give benchmarks to participants for interpretation of events. They bind participants more strongly – at the extreme being political and religious cults that offer little room for disagreement.

Whether general or specific, ideologies constitute the ideational–interpretative component of social organization that serves as the basis for shared goals, common discourse, interpersonal network-based contact, shared identity, and coordination. But we need to be very clear: although the analyst may speak of them in relatively concrete terms, they are constantly in flux as they are socially represented in discourse and action, being debated, discussed, and changed as a movement develops. Some analysts have suggested that this emergent quality is better captured by the concept of frames and framing as an ideational–interpretative accomplishment.

Collective action frames

Since the late 1980s, a large body of research has elaborated the ideational–interpretative dimension of social movements in terms of *collective action frames*. This idea was brought to protest studies as a way of conceptualizing how people break the social-psychological barriers of inaction and conformity to redefine a situation in such a way that they must take a stand (Gamson, Fireman, and Rytina 1982). Because social movements are not established institutions, and because they emerge newly to challenge the status quo, seeking the ideational spark that lies behind their initial appearance is a central task.

As typically used to study protests and campaigns, a frame is a shared cultural construct that gives meaning and direction to collective action by specifying how a situation is to be interpreted (Snow et al. 1986, 2014; Snow and Benford 1988, 1992). Frames are clusters of ideas – some analysts refer to them as schemata – that, as collective representations, guide participants' interpretations of what needs to be changed, how to do it, and why. They direct attention to some aspects of a situation and away from others. Collective action frames can be very specific to movements, such as an "environmental justice frame," a "global justice frame," or an "anti-Wall Street frame." A frame is made up of interrelated concepts that give individual participants ways of seeing the world – through a "global-justice lens" for example, that highlights unfair practices, such as sweatshop production. Frames differ from ideologies because they are not written down and discussed as such, but rather function on the cognitive level of information processing. That said, ideologies are important sources for the material in collective action frames. The two concepts often overlap because articulated ideologies do many of the things that frames do. They give guidelines for perceiving injustice, give motivation for action, and, in Lenin's famous words, answer "What is to be done?" Ideologies help define frames of interpretation and action, but frames are different from ideologies in the sense that they usually function at an unrecognized level of cognition. As collective representations of individual assessments, they are often unarticulated, sometimes functioning subconsciously, but their influence can be seen in how they shape collective action.

Collective interests

Collective interests are typically seen as obvious and not in need of much framing. Most social movements either directly or indirectly pursue the collective interests of their participants. Some social movement analysts, as I will discuss in the next chapter, stress the dominant role of collective interests and the costs of pursuing them in shaping mobilization trajectories, especially when weighed against the interests of established groups who are challenged by social movements. Interests are ideational elements in the sense that they are mental calculations subject to the inaccuracies of the information available, social influences, and emotional states, which all can color their perception and render it quite subjective. Nevertheless, collective interests are often attributed economic and/or political connotations in the sense that calculations of benefits and power are taken as so starkly obvious that little interpretation is needed. We encountered earlier the force of collective interests in the local NIMBY campaign against minidorms. The assumption was that residents who participated saw the threats to neighborhood peace and quiet, property values, and traffic congestion pretty clearly. There was very little ideological elaboration in that group and very little framing of the problem.

It is fair to say that some movements – say, the labor movement or the civil rights movement – have collective interests that play obviously determining roles in mobilizing action, more so than other movements – say, animal liberation or environmentalism. To put it differently, when clearly present, collective interests can have a compelling quality about them, and the space for creative interpretations about the problem and what to do is significantly less. But it also needs to be emphasized that, as human social actors, collective interests are *always interpreted* before action is taken. It cannot be otherwise – it is the interpretative dimension that translates thought into action. When interpretative space is greater, this translation is usually accomplished amidst social influences, taking place in a social group, among others similarly working through shared frames of what is going on and what must be done. In these contexts, the full force of social-psychological factors such as conformity, authority, and collective identity enters in. Without this hiatus between interests and action being bridged by collective interpretations, the researcher does not have a social phenomenon to study. There is no collective action. The question for the researcher is how involved and elaborate is the process of interpretation and how much attention does it warrant.

There is an analytical approach that takes the perspective that it does not warrant much. It is based on the assumptions that interests are starkly evident to individuals, and so are the costs of taking action. Mancur Olson (1963), an economist analyzing labor organizations, suggested that in large collective actions, decisions to participate typically favor not joining – the *free rider* problem, he called it. He reasoned that the rational actor would see that the addition of one more body at a protest probably would not make a difference in the movement's success (attaining *collective goods*, as Olson calls it). Because everyone shares these collective goods if movement goals are attained, the rational actor has no incentive to incur the costs of participating. According to Olson, the way that organizations get people to participate is to offer incentives, which change the balance of costs and benefits in favor of participating. These can be either external (payments or rewards for participating) or internal (feelings of solidarity with others), "hard" or "soft." Olson was an economist, and the cost–benefit lingo of his discipline shapes the analysis into one of rational decisions made by isolated individuals weighing up social movement participation. This economic strand of research has waxed and waned in the development of the social movements field, as I will trace in the next chapter. Suffice it to say here that the kind of movement partly determines the economic emphasis, but also the theoretical lens through which the researcher approaches the movement does too. An emphasis on costs, benefits, and tipping points of collective action is especially strong among some political scientists looking at such action.

Collective identity

In sociology, however, most researchers would not see feelings of solidarity as economic benefits, but rather as the results of social-psychological processes of conformity, shared beliefs, and in-group preferences. All these help define one's individual identity in terms of the social group: its collective identity. Collective identity is recognized as a key factor in why social movements cohere and have continuity over time. In Olson's terms, it is a key internal *solidary incentive* for participation, but in fact it subsumes all the other solidary incentives that an organization might offer, such as friendships, social gatherings, belongingness, solidarity, romantic possibilities, and so on. Collective identity is a key element in a movement's ideational–interpretative dimension because it counterbalances collective interests, and in some instances, overrides them as incentives for participation, as when activists sacrifice for the cause or for their compatriots. It is not surprising then that collective identity has been emphasized as a major element in those contemporary social movements where the pursuit of interests is less clear – in environmentalism and animal rights, for example. Indeed, there are movements where identity is central, as in feminism, animal liberation, or GLBT activism. Thus, in thinking about the ideational dimension of social movements, the balance of interests and collective identity as motivators for action takes a central place. This is a theme that I will explore further in chapters 3 and 4, where I examine political movements and cultural movements regarding the relative weight of interests versus collective identity.

Social Movement Performances

The concept of performance is fundamental to contemporary approaches to culture. The traditional view that reigned in the 1960s was that culture was a web of meaning, embodied in the values, beliefs, attitudes, and predispositions that were widely held throughout the population, interconnected, and all-encompassing. The presumption was that, because all social action is preceded by an idea, knowing how these meanings cluster throughout society gives insights into patterns of behavior. The more widely accepted view today is that, rather than seeing culture solely as a web of meaning, it is also a *web of meaning making* located in the numerous performances that are distributed throughout the social patterns of daily life (Norton 2004; Johnston 2010). This is a perspective that subtly shifts the view of culture from how it is available to individuals as a set of received ideations to how it is created as an ongoing process through performances (Alexander and Mast 2006; Eyerman 2006; Alexander 2011). Norms, values, and beliefs have no impact as long as they are locked in the mental life of individuals, but when they are acted out, others react and help shape the *social representations* that make up culture. The arena of cultural creation is its performance. Swidler (1995) has stressed the performative elements of social movement mobilization by suggesting that social movements draw upon stories, symbols, values, and scripted behaviors and use them selectively, much like a handyman uses tools in his toolbox (see also Lévi-Strauss 1963).

The modern repertoire

Charles Tilly (1995, 2008) played the greatest role in directing analytical attention to the performance aspect of social movements. His research traces how protest patterns have evolved over the last two centuries, such that a widely recognized set of tactics – marches, demonstrations, meetings, petitions, rallies, sit-ins, strikes, and so on – are generally employed today. These forms have taken shape during the nineteenth and twentieth centuries as the modern democratic state has evolved. It is fair to say that democracy and social movements have developed in a reciprocal and mutually reinforcing relationship (Johnston 2011). Today, the performances of marches, demonstrations, and protests constitute part of political culture – namely, how to do politics outside of accepted institutional channels. This modern social movement repertoire is a *strong repertoire* in that its patterns have a compelling cultural quality for activists making choices about how to act. However, a performative perspective also brings to light the emergent component to movement actions in that protesters are always cognizant of their audiences and react to them. Changes in tactical patterns are driven by creative and autonomous participants who innovate as the evolving, real-time protest situation may require. Perhaps the police have been called out in force and occupy an adjacent street, or counterprotesters congeal unexpectedly, which requires a tactical adjustment. Of course, participants may innovate for its own sake – a reflection of their innate creativity – but it is common that improvised performances are influenced by the other players on the scene and by the audience's reaction (e.g., see Murphy 2012).

Networks of performances

In today's most advanced postmodern societies, several theorists (Melucci 1989, 1996; Castells 1996, 1997) have stressed the multiple and overlapping network basis of social movements and their process-oriented, performance-based construction of new meanings. Ideas, oppositional meanings, and symbolism are the sources of energy that animate movement networks (Mische 2003). I close this chapter by observing that it makes sense to think of social movement performances not just in terms of the dramatic theatre of the modern repertoire, but also in terms of small-scale participants' performances that occur in networked relations. Like the grand-scale performances of protest events, many small-scale encounters at meetings, planning sessions, recruitment forays, and socializing also have a performance aspect at the level of interaction. Individuals come together and discuss, debate, assert, narrate, and affirm their positions in smaller social contexts. These are gatherings where meaning is made and remade – just as it is in larger-scale performances. Their network basis also means that some performative situations will have more participants than others, and/or will be more significant and central in meaning production for the movement.

Obviously the big marches and demonstrations that mobilize thousands are critical in defining the movement for its participants as well as for their audiences. But what the movement means to its participants is crucial for mobilizing these large protests, and small organizational meetings and coffee-shop gatherings where movement ideas are discussed, elaborated, and "performed" are locales where rationales and motivations for action are grounded. At any given moment, a social movement is composed of a vast matrix of big and small performances. The big ones may be highly significant in the movement's self-definition (and especially in its definition for outsiders), but the smaller ones are the multitudinous building blocks of a movement's structure and its ideations. It is through these performances, big and small, that the movement becomes what it is for its participants and for its opponents and audiences. It is where movement culture is created and confirmed. To put it another way, not only is a social movement made up of a network of relatively fixed relations among SMOs, groups, and individuals, but also it is a dense network of performances, macro and micro, through which both the structural sphere and the ideational–interpretative sphere are acted out real time. In this sense, the performative sphere can be thought of as being densely networked too.

Conclusion

There is a traditional Chinese saying: the beginning of knowledge is to call things by their right name. In many ways this idea serves as the justification for a book built on the question "What is a social movement?" Let us see if we can draw together the various threads that have been woven into the fabric of this chapter to present a comprehensive and practical definition.

The social movement concept is a high-level abstraction that embraces complex sociocultural phenomena whose boundaries, ideally, are drawn by how three basic dimensions of social life converge: (1) the structural–organizational sphere; (2) shared ideational and interpretative elements; and (3) networked performances that confirm, elaborate, and give life to the first two. In a general sense, this convergence should define a social movement in terms of SMOs that make it up, their social-change goals, and their repertoire of protests, marches, strikes, and so on, so that similarities between one movement and another should be immediately apparent. At the same time, movements should stand out as sufficiently different from related phenomena, such as formally structured NGOs, lobbying organizations, political parties, or general cultural trends with minimal organizational basis.

The social world does not clearly categorize itself like in physics and chemistry. Sometimes analysts approach social movement phenomena from the margins because they give insight about relevant processes and relationships, or they may be interested in the gray areas themselves – the intersection of institutional politics and social movements, for example. Yet because the study of social movements is not physics, it is important that we define our terms carefully and precisely, something every good social scientist is acutely aware of. Let us see if we can do that here.

1. Social movements collectively pursue *social change goals*, derived from ideologies, interests, and frames that define a problem as warranting action. Some movements mobilize against change – say, the anti-abortion movement in the US or anti-gay coalitions – but the vast majority pursue progressive ideals of social and economic justice.
2. Social movement performances mostly follow the modern repertoire of marches, sit-ins, protest actions, demonstrations, picketing, meetings, rallies, and so on. These are *extrainstitutional actions* to influence decision makers. For some SMOs, a mix of strategies is not uncommon, however, which can take the analyst into the gray area of more institutionally focused political contention.
3. Social movements are structurally diverse, made up of *numerous, networked groups, organizations, and individual adherents*. They are not just one large SMO. This diverse, networked quality differentiates social movements, broadly defined, from more bounded phenomena such as interest groups, NIMBY groups, advocacy organizations, focused protest campaigns, and so on.
4. Social movements have *cohesion and continuity* over time, partly derived from their organizational breadth

that comes from their networked structure, as described in point 3.

5. This continuity is also partly based on a movement's *collective identity*, an ideational–interpretative element that is conformed and elaborated in numerous small-scale microperformances that also constitute a movement.

For the beginning student, points 1 and 2 – broad social change goals and the unique repertoire of marches, demonstrations, and protests – set the defining boundaries of what a social movement is. For the professional social scientist, points 3 through 5 pose the key theoretical questions: as collective actions, first, where do they come from, and, second, how do they cohere? How are these examples of complex noninstitutional – that is, new, emergent, and often unexpected – social organization possible? And, finally, why are some successful and others not? These are the key questions to be answered in the chapters that follow as we explore further what a social movement is and how the study of social movements is accomplished.

2
The Study of Social Movements

This chapter tells a story of how an important field of study in the social sciences, one that spans sociology, political science, and social psychology, grew to maturity in the last half-century. In the United States, its adolescence was tumultuous, commencing amidst the numerous protests and social movements of the 1960s. The movements of that decade kindled widespread research attention to collective action, protest, social-change groups and their organization, and inspired a generation of scholars to systematically and empirically study these phenomena. Researchers sought to explain the black civil rights movement, the movement against the war in Vietnam, the women's movement, environmentalism, the Chicano movement, the new age movement, the hippie movement, student political radicalism, and political violence.

There is a related story that will be also told in these pages: the honing of the tools of social science to study social movements and protest. In the 1960s, theorizing about collective behavior and social movements was less grounded in empirical research. At its best, it was based on systematic observation, informed reasoning, and logical deductions about causes and connections among apparently related phenomena. Many of the ideas were good ones, but that by itself does not make social science. This chapter traces how a field of research came of age as a community of scholars worked to refine theory using increasingly sophisticated research tools. In the US, a critical mass of social movement researchers was reached sometime around the mid-1970s, and their concepts, findings, methods, and debates took off exponentially thereafter. Today, the study of protests, social movements, and contentious politics is a major research focus in both North America and Europe, and its influence continues to grow.

It is crucial to understand this period because the fundamental orientations that define social movement research today were mostly evident in these formative years. They were present in simpler, less nuanced and elaborated forms, but their basic truths remain. Of course, the bad ideas of the period – say, notions of some sort of "group mind" that sweeps participants away or the emotional irrationality of protesters – have been discarded, but the good ones have persisted. In the broadest sense, key among these was the insight that social movements and protest activism are not extraordinary phenomena, but rather are behaviors much closer to everyday political, economic, and cultural life than had been previously thought. Although recognition of this was slow, the effect was to pull the study of social movements from the realms of the obscure and bizarre – popular fads like the hula-hoop and deviant groups like flying saucer cults – and weave it throughout the normal fabric of everyday political and social processes. As such, the field was better positioned to show its relevance and prosper by drawing connections with other disciplines and proving its credentials to new generations of scholars.

So, once upon a time, when sociology was just becoming established as an academic field (in the mid nineteenth century), and a century before the events mentioned above, there was a French psychologist named Gustave Le Bon. He wrote a book called *The Crowd: A Study of the Popular Mind* (1894) that became fashionable among academics and political elites of the period. At that time, the revolutions of 1848 were not too distant in historical memory, and working-class protests, strikes, and union campaigns were causing widespread disruption. Le Bon's ideas were strongly influenced by psychological concepts popular at that time, such as unconscious processes, regression to childhood patterns, and irrational libidinous influences on behavior. He proposed that when the masses act collectively, the overwhelming influence of the group causes a decrease in individual judgment. He treated crowds as unified actors that generated a mind of their own – a *group mind* – with the tendency to overwhelm individual discernment and make people more susceptible to unconscious influences. In everyday parlance, such ideas are still to be found. The popular media sometime speaks of being "swept away by the crowd," a common phrase that captures Le Bon's thinking and stereotypical explanations of why protesting crowds often turn unruly and violent.

As I write these words, media reports covering rampaging crowds throwing rocks and setting fires, destroying property, and attacking police lines crowd the daily papers and evening news. While protest gatherings sometimes turn unruly, it is important to be very clear on this account: the vast majority of social movements today mobilize without any instances of violence, nor any evidence of a group mind, compulsive contagion, or loss of discernment. Rather, most take the form of marches, demonstrations, strikes, or protest rallies, occur through organization and planning, and are far from spontaneously irrational actions. Le Bon's ideas are resoundingly rejected by social movement researchers today. When violence occurs, it is safe to generalize that it is a result either of police actions that precipitate a spiral of confrontation, or of consciously planned tactics of a subgroup within the a larger protest gathering. Violent confrontations in the huge wave of anti-austerity protests that occurred between 2008 and 2011 were mostly the result of these two factors (Johnston and Seferiades 2012).

Collective Behavior

I opened with Le Bon's book because, in the historiography of protest studies, it contained the first pen strokes of a line of demarcation that ran through the study of social movements for many years. On one side of the line, researchers conceived collective acts of protest as extraordinary events that were fundamentally irrational, as Le Bon would have it. On this side too was a related approach that conceptualized them as reflections of some kind of collective pathology, deviance, or social breakdown, which implied that psychological instability and susceptibility led people to participation in social movements. The argument went this way: if society failed to provide opportunities for its citizens, or to integrate them civically and morally, then anger, frustration, and aggression would build and collective outbursts of protest and rage would occur.

On the other side of the fault line, when violence and militant disruption occur, they may be seen as merely tactics intentionally chosen to achieve a collective goal, or sensible responses to unfolding developments on the ground, for example when the police attack protesters. More generally, in this line of thinking, social movements occur as people make perfectly rational and understandable claims against unresponsive authorities, or defend collective interests against other groups – in other words, they are an extension of normal political contention. Moreover, successful movements are those that can organize, strategize, plan, and astutely apply the resources at their disposal to the mobilizing tasks at hand – that is, the fundamental task of getting people up and into the streets. This interpretation does a much better job of accounting for the fact I just mentioned – that most social movement actions are not unruly and disruptive – and is a view that gives major direction to the social movements field today. Although emotions are certainly present in protest gatherings, and a body of literature has sought to bring them back into the study of mobilization processes (Goodwin, Jasper, and Polletta 2004; Flam and King 2005; Gould 2002, 2009), they do not occupy a place of primary causation in the broad panorama of current research. As we will see in later chapters, this may be to the detriment of a full understanding, but, for now, the point is that positioning oneself on one side of the fault line or the other may inappropriately exclude relevant factors.

This fundamental division between rationality and irrationality has given rise to its own terminology: the label *collective behavior* was traditionally applied to actions viewed through the irrational lens, while the term *collective action* is usually used with the presumption of rationality behind the action. If terminological usage is a rough measure of a field's orientation, one does not hear much about collective behavior these days, and the label *collective action* is claimed by highly mathematical, formal analyses done mostly in political science. The current watchword is *contentious politics*, which embraces rational organization and strategic planning, and stresses how social movement mobilization is mostly politics by another means. This chapter lays out the road map that traces how the field got to this point; the next chapter explores the contentious politics perspective in depth. Although this black-and-white way of seeing the development of perspectives on social movements glosses a good deal of detail, it is a useful starting place to consider the field's evolution. It also gives insights into the topography of the field today.

The Chicago School

At about the same time that Le Bon's ideas were enjoying popularity in the salons of Europe, American sociology was developing its own distinctive orientation at the University of Chicago. At the outset of the twentieth century, sociology was just emerging as an academic discipline. As we saw with Le Bon, who was influenced by Freudian psychology, what became known as the Chicago School of sociology was influenced by other disciplines: the behaviorist psychology of John Watson, the pragmatist philosophy of John Dewey, and the social behaviorism of G. H. Mead – all of whom were at the University of Chicago. Because of sociology's emergent status, these concentrations of scholars were important influences. Pragmatism was a school of philosophy that stressed the problem-solving nature of human behavior and everyday ideas and beliefs as the focus of philosophical inquiry. Combining the empirical focus of behaviorist psychology with pragmatism's focus on everyday problem-solving, a new and unique perspective emerged in American sociology that came to be called "symbolic interactionism." It also became the distinctive stamp of the Chicago School's approach to collective behavior.

The essence of Chicago School sociology was codified in Robert Park and Ernest Burgess's *An Introduction to the Science of Sociology* (1969 [1921]). Their chapter on collective behavior drew heavily on Le Bon's view of crowds as examples of irrational and primordial behaviors. In one subsection of that chapter, Park and Burgess discuss "animal crowds," observing that human crowds begin with a similar "milling process," where goals are absent but a mutual responsiveness develops among participants, which diminishes their self-control and renders them more susceptible to suggestion. In Park and Burgess's view, collective behavior was both irrational and distinct from forms of everyday social interaction. Although their chapter considers examples of social movements, they are not systematically analyzed as distinct forms of collective behavior, but rather grouped with other out-of-the-ordinary social forms.

Herbert Blumer was another University of Chicago sociologist, and really the godfather of symbolic interactionism in the United States. In fact, he coined the term to reflect its emphasis on meaning construction and social process. Symbolic interactionism is a theoretical focus that remains alive and well today in American sociology – less so in political science. It focuses on the processual, emergent, and meaningful qualities of social life, with a strong social-psychological orientation that emerged from Chicago's pragmatist focus on the small, everyday tasks of social life. For early symbolic interactionists, explaining collective behavior became an especially compelling question because it represented such a break from everyday concerns.

Blumer (1951) explains how social movements develop by beginning with the gradual coalescence of crowds, first through dissatisfaction and agitation spreading among a group, which becomes the basis of shared awareness. Next, a "we consciousness" develops to give definition to the coalescing group. In Blumer's language, an "esprit de corps" develops to provide group solidarity and a sense of belonging that becomes part of the members' self-identity. Next, group morale develops, based on convictions of rectitude and correctness of demands. Upon this base, an organization coalesces, which more clearly specifies the group's demands and tactics. Think back to chapter 1 and the discussion of the NIMBY movement against minidorms near my university. Blumer's descriptive approach to social movement formation captures some of the processes at work in the development of a neighborhood group such as this. All this said, Blumer's perspective, starting as it does from scratch and tracing the process of gradual coalescence, misses a fundamental finding that has emerged in social movement research: protest actions grow out of pre-existing organizations and not through a general coming-together process based on disconnected and discontented people milling around.

Concerns about the conditions of emergence and the extraordinary quality of protests remained a theme of symbolic interactionist approaches, most notably studies done under the banner of *collective behavior* perspectives. The ideas of Ralph Turner and Lewis Killian (1987 [1957]) built upon the Chicago School – interactionist approaches but questioned assumptions about the uniformity, goal-directedness, and emotional character of crowds. They proposed that crowds and movement groups are really quite diverse and that the nonordinary quality of their behavior, as well as the apparent uniformity that they exhibit, are explained by the concept of new *emergent norms* (Turner 1996). The idea is that participants are never completely disassociated from their ordinary lives where accepted social norms guide behaviors. Under circumstances in which aspects of one's life become problematic, people are temporarily guided by emergent norms. These are new guidelines for appropriate behavior that address new life circumstances, and which give shape to the extraordinary behaviors characteristic of protests, demonstrations, and even outbreaks of collective violence. They evolve from the interaction within the crowd and emergent definitions among participants of what they are doing and how far they should go. Participants experience pressure to conform to the new emergent norms – social conformity being a basic social-psychological process that can be transferred to extraordinary social phenomena such as protests and demonstrations. To the outside observer, this helps explain the veneer of uniform action that is apparent in phenomena as diverse as crowds, riots, crazes, general shifts in public opinion, and social movements.

Breakdown Theories

A different branch of collective behaviorism grew from the second great center of American sociology at Harvard University, under the influence of Talcott Parsons, the foremost theorist of structural functionalism in the mid twentieth century. Neil Smelser, Parsons's student and later Professor of Sociology at University of California, Berkeley, wrote *Theory of Collective Behavior* in 1962. Reminiscent of Parsons's theories of social action, Smelser's book is a systematic-yet-abstract schema of interrelated determinants that aims at a high level of generalization. His theory included phenomena as diverse as panics, crazes, hostile outbursts, reform movements, and revolutionary movements under one conceptual umbrella, the assumption being that the same factors are at work in all these collective forms. Smelser's theory specified six necessary and sufficient determinants: structural conduciveness, structural strain, the spread of generalized beliefs, a precipitating event that sets off the collective behavior, mobilization for action, and the overarching counterforce of social control and how it constrains the development of action.

True to Smelser's structural-functionalist roots, he emphasizes the centrality of structural influences, most notably structural conduciveness, structural strain, and social control. These determinants shift the focus of analysis from interactive processes characteristic of the Chicago School, to structural problems at the societal level and, then, how the individual integrates his or her action according to different levels of social action. This reconciliation of individual action with social structure is perhaps where Parsons's influence is most strongly felt. From general to specific, individual behaviors are guided and coordinated at the broadest level by society's values as general orientations to action. Then, more specifically, actions are guided by social norms appropriate to given situations. Then, even more specifically, "motivations for organized action" guide behaviors within groups. Finally, "situational facilities" represent specific adjustments to small-scale, immediate social situations. Smelser suggests that, when a person experiences structural strain, he or she acts at one of these levels to compensate for it. If many people act in the same way, we get collective behavior. Depending on the level at which the response is focused, different forms of collective behavior occur. For example, people can act to change society's basic value structures. If they do, we get a broad revolutionary movement. But if people experience social strain or tension and act only on the level of the immediate situation – "situational facilities" in Parsons's terminology – that is, among their friends and immediate associates, the result may be a popular craze. The assumption is that crazes, which might be fun or confirm group belong-ingness, reduce experiences of structural strain on an immediate, psychological level. In this way, Smelser lumps together in one broad theoretical scheme phenomena as diverse as rapidly spreading fads – dancing the Macarena or young men wearing their pants below their backsides – and Egypt's popular uprising in spring 2011.

Few researchers in social movements today make these kinds of conceptual leaps, but in the 1960s such connec-tions were widely taken for granted, representing a view of all forms of collective behavior as non-normative, excep-tional, and destabilizing. We see this from a different angle if we consider what have come to be called *breakdown approaches* to social movements. In the 1950s and 1960s, the breakdown perspective was strongly conditioned by the rise of right-wing McCarthyism, segregationist opposition to civil rights in the US, and social science thinking about European fascist movements, which were still in recent memory at that time. The classics in this genre drew heavily on the European experience: Ortega y Gasset's *Revolt of the Masses* (1932), Mannheim's *Man and Society in an Age of Reconstruction* (1940), and Arendt's *The Origins of Totalitarianism* (1951), all of which focused on the political consequences of urban-industrial society, with a strong psy-chological emphasis on individual adaptation and integra-tion. This focus shifted scholarly attention away from fads, crazes, and riots, and similar forms of apolitical action, and situated the study of social movements in the political realm, where many practitioners today prefer to dwell – more on this shortly.

Kornhauser's *The Politics of Mass Society* (1959) offered a theoretical synthesis of the breakdown perspective from American experience. He noted that, in modern society, the informal centers of group attachment are replaced by impersonal and bureaucratic relations. Urbanization and industrialization have weakened primary "intermediate" associations such as family, class, community, and ethnic bonds. With the dispersion of middle-range mechanisms of authority and integration, the modern citizen of mass society is left isolated, detached, and anomic. In the context of democratic participation, modern citizens are prone to recruitment by mass political movements. "By divorcing people from larger social purposes, mass society also tends to separate people from themselves," Kornhauser writes (1959: 107). Drawing on Chicago School ideas of suggestibility, he proposes that people alienated from the social order are alienated from themselves and psychologically susceptible to recruitment from mass appeals.

Although Kornhauser focuses on political movements, his model shares with Smelser's several basic elements: social strain or breakdown, individual alienation to explain protesters' availability, and a leadership (guided by an integrating ideological system – Smelser's "generalized beliefs") which stirs participants to action. In the context of the Cold War, scholars applied variants of these ingredients to explain movements typical of the 1950s and 1960s: political violence, domestic unrest, insurgencies, revolutions, and communist-inspired national liberation movements in the developing world. The key reflection of structural imbalance or breakdown in these treatments was the concept of relative deprivation, a psychological state experienced by citizens when society does not deliver on the social and economic aspirations it has created.

Deprivation, Frustration, and Aggression

In the post-war period, collective violence and civil unrest became hot topics in the social sciences. Within sociology, there was interest in the protests and urban riots that occurred in the 1960s in the context of African-American claims and the anti-Vietnam war movement. Also, New Left student movements mobilized widely in the US and Europe, including vanguards of small revolutionary groups that initiated violent actions against the state and establishment targets. In political science, there was a thread of research that focused on international comparisons, especially of anticolonial liberation movements and insurgencies against the state. After the end of World War II, numerous movements, frequently animated by Marxism–Leninism, Maoism, and/or nationalism, erupted against weakened European colonial administrations. In the context of the Cold War, researchers sought explanations for these movements, some drawing upon notions of social breakdown caused by rapid modernization, and others elaborating the concept of relative deprivation.

In the 1960s, the term *the revolution of rising expectations* was commonly invoked to explain not only the attraction of communism in many underdeveloped countries but also the rise of insurgencies and revolutionary movements. James C. Davies (1969) used the French, American, Russian, and Mexican Revolutions to illustrate his J-curve hypothesis, a formal model of the relationships among rising expectations, their level of satisfaction, and revolutionary upheavals. He proposed that revolution is likely when, after a long period of rising expectations accompanied by a parallel increase in their satisfaction, a downturn occurs. When perceptions of satisfaction decrease but expectations do not, an unsustainable gap widens between the two. This is an analysis based on the social psychology of individual perceptions that are aggregated into widespread public sentiments. The widening gap precipitates a rebellion against a social system that fails to fulfill its promises. The Cuban Revolution in 1959, the leftist insurgency in the Dominican Republic (1965), and several leftist guerrilla movements in South America (Venezuela, Colombia, Bolivia) were attributed to such unfulfilled expectations. At the heart of this model's social psychology is a logic of collective frustration arising from unfulfilled expectations leading to aggressive behavior manifested in political rebellion, civil unrest, or protest campaigns.

The idea that unfulfilled expectations create unstable social and political situations is closely related to the variable of relative deprivation as an explanation of civil unrest. Relative deprivation is the perceived discrepancy between what people think they should achieve and what they have indeed achieved. It was the animating concept of a large body of research – Ted Robert Gurr (1970) being perhaps the best-known practitioner – to explain not only uprisings internationally, but also domestic civil unrest. As the theory goes, the early successes of the civil rights movement in the 1950s raised expectations among American blacks, but their subsequent dissatisfaction with the slow pace of change during the 1960s was seen as a cause of urban riots in the US (Geshwender 1964; Runciman 1966). Applying this idea to civil unrest there, several studies showed that rioting occurred in cities where improvement of conditions for blacks was greatest.

Most research along these lines, on both urban riots and comparative political violence, used objective macroeconomic measures to infer deprivation – for example, rising GNP or regional occupational patterns that were matched with periods of mobilization and protest. However, because relative deprivation is an individual psychological assessment, conclusive proof of its influence requires more. Survey and interview data that gave insight into participants' state of mind sometimes found that the relationship between deprivation and protest was not strong (McPhail 1971; Abeles 1976), or that people were much more pragmatic about future expectations than data for economic trends suggested (Oberschall 1968). These findings indicated that other variables were at work behind social movement occurrence, most notably how individual psychological states get translated into collective action – the process of mobilizing people to actually get into the streets. Because of these criticisms, and especially because of subsequent research findings about the crucial role of organizational, political, and recruitment processes, most social movement scholars today deemphasize relative deprivation, rising expectations, and collective frustration, at least in sociology.

Normalizing Protest

Our narrative is now in the late 1960s and early 1970s, that period when the number of scholars focusing on social movements increased significantly, a reflection of the turbulent times in both national and international arenas. In the field of social movements, a critical mass of young scholars coalesced around new theoretical insights that challenged the extraordinary character of protest movements. In sociology, these scholars were William Gamson, Charles Tilly, Anthony Oberschall, John McCarthy, Mayer Zald, John Lofland, Roberta Ash, Jo Freeman, Gary Marx, and others. A few years later, the list grew longer as some of their students, plus others from political science and social psychology, entered the chain reaction. The result was an explosion of research that turned away from relative deprivation and mass society approaches, and which occurred mostly in the discipline of sociology.

Much of this new research focused on the interests of challenging groups, and how these groups and organizations successfully mobilize to make their claims. The most compelling and enduring insight was that social movements and protest were not unusual phenomena but rather reflections of normal social, economic, and political processes. Various themes and approaches related to this point of view came to be loosely categorized under the label of the *resource mobilization perspective* (or simply RM). They all shared a rejection of frustration, deprivation, and mass society as causes of protest movements, and the recognition that organization and strategy were critical for success. Most observers of the field would agree that the richness of the RM perspective, plus a new methodological sophistication, plus the intense political drama of the 1960s and 1970s combined to launch the social movement studies field toward its current status as a major research focus in sociology. Although many of RM's concepts have subsequently been elaborated and channeled in different directions, its fundamental tenets remain to this day in various incarnations.

One of the early participants in this critical mass was Anthony Oberschall. His book *Social Conflict and Social*

Movements (1973) contrasted with mass society and relative deprivation perspectives by arguing that organization was the key to social movement mobilization. Oberschall's direct challenge to the mass society hypothesis was his finding that participation was usually the result of group membership via bloc recruitment. He observed that, rather than as disconnected individual citizens manipulated by leaders, people join movements as members of groups. Using a fundamental dichotomy from social theory, he distinguished, first, traditionally based communal groups founded on local ties, culture, and/or religious identity, and, second, civic groups, characteristic of modern social organization, which reflect common interests and contractual relations. Also, he suggested that the kinds of groups that mobilized participants could be analyzed in terms of their internal and external social linkages. Strong internal group cohesion increases the probability that the group in its entirety can be mobilized to action, and reduces the costs of doing so. Groups with varied external linkages are moderated by crosscutting interests and ties and, Oberschall suggested, are less prone to mobilization.

Oberschall's emphasis on mobilizing organizations helped solve a fundamental problem of collective action suggested several years earlier by economist Mancur Olson (1963). Recall our discussion of Olson's ideas in chapter 1. If attained, *collective goods* are enjoyed not only by active social movement participants, but also by nonparticipant *free riders*. For example, civil rights protests in the American South broke segregation for all blacks, not just those who risked life and limb to march and protest. Olson observed that, for a totally rational decision maker, it does not make sense to participate in groups seeking collective goods. Let others do the work (incur the costs of protests) and you get the benefits anyway – the *free rider problem*. This is compounded the larger groups get, because potential participants will quickly realize that the addition of one more person won't make much of a difference.

Olson observed that groups could solve this problem by providing "selective incentives" that raise the benefits for participants, making their participation more likely. Selective incentives may be "hard" like money or gifts, or "soft" like camaraderie and collective identity. Going back to Ober-schall's findings about pre-existing organizations, communal groups and those organizations that do not have external overlaps in membership are better able to provide such "soft" incentives of identity and social support. They are precisely the kind of organization that can demand a lot of its members because they give back a lot in terms of collective identification and solidarity. Regarding "harder" incentives, organizations need resources – and especially financial resources – to provide these more costly kinds of benefits. This is where the "resource" in the resource mobilization perspective comes in. It opens up a different perspective on mobilization, but still one based on organization and the economics of the decision to participate.

The Economic Metaphor

John McCarthy and Mayer Zald were RM theorists who emphasized organizational and economic influences in social movement mobilization. They began by observing a basic paradox during the turbulent 1960s: a rising trend of activism during a time of unparalleled economic prosperity (Zald 2010: 252). If relative deprivation and frustration–aggression theories were correct, this should not be the case: post-war economic trends of greater affluence and greater income equality would predict a decrease in social movement activity. According to McCarthy and Zald (1977), this paradox is resolved by the idea that greater affluence means that contending groups have more resources available to get their message out to the public and to mobilize participants into the streets. They argue that movement mobilization is linked to organizational structure, material resources, cost reduction, strategic planning, and the professionalization of movement activists, especially among the upper-level strategists in large movement organizations whom they call *social movement entrepreneurs*. All these observations elaborate and extend Oberschall's challenge to mass society theory, offering further confirmation that it was through organization that people participated in social movements, not as a result of their disconnectedness and anomie. They also situate the study of social movements in the structural sphere by paying primary attention to organizational processes.

By stressing processes that one finds in rationally structured, complex organizations, the RM perspective further dispelled the emphasis on deprivation, aggression, and frustration. It did this by proposing that, in contemporary societies, everybody has a gripe, so to speak. Affluent societies are permeated with competing interests, unfulfilled aspirations, grievances, demands, and claims. All groups have claims and interests to pursue. This means that grievances and demands are not unusual and, in a sense, are held constant across contentious groups and organizations. Thus, it is not the strength of the claims but something else that *really* explains social movement mobilization. Here McCarthy and Zald provided an answer: the ability of groups to procure resources, get their messages out, and mobilize their members into the streets. Taking this a step further – perhaps cynically, but supported by the campaigns of the largest SMOs – McCarthy and Zald state: "the definition of grievances will expand to meet the funds and support personnel available" (1973: 379).

When I speak of resources, I mean primarily money – hard cash to support staff, organization, and offices, pay for phones and communication, print flyers and signs, transport protesters, etc. The bare-bones observation – a useful oversimplification really – is that groups with more money are more likely to mobilize participants and to have an impact on public opinion. Where numerous interests compete in the public forum, and where groups and organizations frequently mobilize over political issues, resource availability becomes the crucial factor in explaining mobilization (hence, *resource mobilization*). Resource-rich groups can effectively get out their message, organize activists, and influence the public and political representatives. This is true in political campaigns as it is in protest campaigns . . . most of the time, that is. While the importance of resources is an enduring finding, it is important to recognize that there are instances when the compelling nature of a grievance, claim, or wrong inflicted can thrust a resource-poor organization into the limelight and/or trump the deep pockets of opposing interests. Because resources are quantifiable, in the broad sweep of the field's development this had methodological implications that tended to direct attention away from concepts such as ideologies, emergent perception of interests and norms, and social-psychological processes of interpretation and social construction. Researchers could concentrate on hard data about concrete structural factors. While it is fair to say that this shift went a long way in granting legitimacy to the new field of research, it also tended to inhibit research interest in the ideational sphere of movements.

Procuring resources and putting them to use effectively are closely connected with good management of SMOs. McCarthy and Zald (1977) were also the first to discern this trend back in the 1970s: namely, mobilization strategy and planning were becoming increasingly rationalized and professionalized. As mentioned in chapter 1, large movement organizations increasingly emphasized resource procurement through specialization and professionalization. As they formally structure their organizations to maximize efficiency, they sometimes take on the characteristics of private corporations and the state. As we saw, SMOs can be huge, multinational organizations that pursue mass marketing campaigns to attract "checkbook members," people whose support of a cause is mostly demonstrated by paying membership fees.

If all this seems to the reader to be one big economic enterprise, Zald and McCarthy were in agreement. Their analysis intentionally used several economic metaphors (Zald and McCarthy 1987) to describe the contemporary social movement scene. For example, like industries that offer similar products (e.g., the steel industry, the consumer electronics industry, the automobile industry), *social movement industries* were made up of large SMOs with similar goals (e.g., environmental conservation, human rights, global economic justice). Like corporations, SMOs sometimes had interlocking boards of directors and developed alliances, cartels, mergers, and joint ventures. And as I discussed in chapter 1, some SMOs market their memberships like products, tailoring their recruitment messages (advertisements) to target audiences. This synergy between large SMOs and corporations was a key discovery of McCarthy and Zald that reflected a new trend in the *social movement sector* – another of their economic metaphors, by the way, like the manufacturing sector, financial sector, or service sector – but it represented one dimension of the broader theoretical shift occurring under the RM umbrella. The other dimension fostered the recognition that social movement mobilization and protest are but other ways of doing politics.

Social Movements as Contentious Politics

In 1975 the term *contentious politics* was not yet fashionable, but it is a label that is widely used today to capture how social movements and disruptive protest are often politics by another means. In 1975, this view was just emerging. In contrast to electoral campaigns and political party competition, taking to the streets to protest against a policy or vocalize a claim is a more challenging, in-your-face way of pursuing group interests. I conclude this chapter by pointing out that the roots of today's contentious-politics focus go back to the RM period of the 1970s, and especially the work of two seminal scholars, William Gamson and Charles Tilly. They were instrumental in shifting the field away from RM's original economic and corporate-organizational imagery and toward its continuity with normal politics. It was a shift that also functioned to mainstream the field to a greater extent, attracting more scholars in political science and political sociology.

Gamson's research came at RM issues from a slightly different angle, but its overall effect was to give strong empirical support to the view that protest was a normal political act. His study *The Strategy of Social Protest* (1975; a second edition was published in 1990) presented evidence that choosing to protest, and especially employing extremist measures and violent tactics, are strategic decisions made by challenging groups. In 1975, this finding went a long way to put to rest the lingering irrationalist biases from earlier in our story. But also the study's basic research question was directed at elements of pluralist political theory, which was the operative framework among political scientists for understanding how democratic political competition is peacefully accomplished. Pluralism refers to multiple centers of interest in a democratic regime, which, because of numerous and overlapping memberships, preclude a winner-take-all approach to governance and associated risks to civil order. According to the standard version of pluralist theory, this was the "genius of democracy," numerous and overlapping memberships added up to a fundamental mechanism by which groups moderated their claims and abided by the rules of the game to contribute to peaceful resolution of conflicting political interests.

If this is the case, Gamson asked, why is it that interest groups and associations sometimes go outside peaceful political channels and resort to extremist strategies and violence? Although Gamson is a sociologist, this was eminently a question that interested political scientists, and went a long way to bridge the two disciplines in the early period. His study was a systematic and empirically grounded approach. He sampled 53 voluntary groups for the period 1800 to 1945, some of which were SMOs, some party organizations, some socialist groups, some unions, and others interest groups (e.g., League of American Wheelmen, American Federation of Teachers). The key criterion for selection was that a group had made a disruptive challenge or claim on behalf of its constituents. The analysis was based on a systematic review of group histories on multiple dimensions – tactics, membership, claims, outcomes, organization, legislative ties and strategies, official repression, among other variables.

The study constructed a database that allowed examination of several concepts that were fundamental in the RM perspective. Most importantly, it laid to rest past visions of the "unruly mob." Gamson found that groups that used extremist tactics had better rates of success. They had both their immediate claims answered and better chances of gaining legitimacy in the eyes of political elites. Moreover, he found little evidence that such tactics injured long-term prospects for the group. He argued that extremism is a strategic choice resulting from a group's position in the political environment, and that groups denied access to channels of political influence may find violent protest to be an effective strategy to win concessions. In Gamson's words, "In place of the old duality of extremist politics and pluralist politics, there is simply politics" (1990 [1975]: 138), an elegant statement that recast social movements as simply politics by another means.

Charles Tilly, a prolific historical social scientist, was also an early sculptor of this politically themed strand of RM theory. His historical scholarship is complex, nuanced, yet also theoretical, systematic, and strongly embedded in the concepts of the field's critical mass period. In 1978, he brought together several strands of his thinking into a theoretical-historical treatise entitled *From Mobilization to Revolution.* As the title states, he moves from the basic components of how collective action gets mobilized to historical examples in various states, most notably England and France, and then to the ultimate challenge that activists pose to the state: revolutionary insurrections. He defines the concept of mobilization in RM terms, as groups laying hold of the resources needed for collective action, and elaborates an RM perspective on organization by identifying features that facilitate the mobilization task. Tilly accepts and builds upon Oberschall's insights about group ties and bloc recruitment by identifying two basic elements of organization: category and network. "Category" refers to ethnic, gender, locality, class, or religious definitions of membership. "Network" refers to the interpersonal bonds among members. These are the two fundamental dimensions of social organization. In Tilly's reckoning, organization = category x network, both of which determine mobilization potential. Putting both together, Tilly suggests that an organization's *catnet* is directly related to how it can lay claim to member resources. High *catnet* – because of higher solidarity, collective identification, and commitment – means an organization can mobilize resources more easily (Tilly 1978: 63). These threads of analysis firmly identify Tilly's early RM credentials.

Yet Tilly's key contribution at this time was how he incorporated insights that RM theorists had neglected, most notably the role of the state – how it shapes opportunities to act – and the organization of the polity, defined as the broad array of political players and nonplayers. Interest in this second group – those excluded from the political game – is central to the field's focus because: (1) their entry as energized players threatens the status quo; and (2) explaining how their entry occurs goes to the heart of the mobilization problem. Following Gamson, challengers must strategize, organize, and mobilize to have their interest-driven claims taken seriously. Major challenges to political elites will be taken as dire threats to their power and invoke strong repression from the police, military, and security forces. It is not surprising then that groups that seek to displace political elites – as in revolutionary movements – are often targets of the most severe and intense state repression.

These themes point forward to the next chapter that looks closely at the synthetic political opportunity model of collective action, often subsumed under the label of *contentious politics*. Here it is enough to note that Tilly laid out its basic contours by specifying how political opportunities vary among different civic organizations according to how they are situated in the polity. Obviously, politically connected groups and organizations have greater opportunities to pursue and protect their interests using established channels. Connected groups also tend to have greater resources and therefore greater power, and must be taken seriously by other groups and organizations. The effect is to bring the study of social movements closer to normal politics.

In contrast, challenges from groups that lie outside the polity usually always threaten established elites and invoke responses from the state. This embeds their extraordinariness in the context of the state, and, again, draws linkages back to normal politics. Tilly hypothesizes that two elements affect the state's response to an organization's claims: (1) the scale of collective action that it can mobilize, as a reflection of its potential threat; and (2) its power, as a reflection of its political opportunities (Tilly 1978: 133). Powerful groups will probably not face repression from the state when they mobilize, and, indeed, may even enjoy state support – a condition that Tilly calls *facilitation* – but this presumes political connections. On the other hand, the greater the scale of collective action – the larger the protests and/or demonstrations – the more likely the state will respond with repression, unless the acting groups enjoy a degree of power – say, through coalitions with connected groups. The bottom line is that the mix of power and numbers determines the kind of response from the state, ranging from repression to tolerance to facilitation.

Power and numbers (and resources) are quantifiable variables in movement development and in their outcomes. We began this chapter with the observation that a parallel narrative of the critical mass period was the development of greater methodological sophistication in the field. The research projects of Gamson and Tilly were based on empirically focused and sophisticated methodological protocols. When published, they were both accompanied by huge methodological appendices at the end of each book. Today, Gamson and Tilly are iconic in social movement research, but, during the critical mass period, they were young scholars establishing their credibility in an emerging field. But it is also fair to say that, during the critical mass period, the sophistication of their studies helped establish the credibility *of* an emerging field. Moreover, this methodological sophistication went a long way to situate the study of social movement in the broader enterprise of social science and strengthened its linkages with political scientists and with social psychologists. Gamson's next book, *Encounters with Unjust Authority* (Gamson et al. 1982), was a classic in social psychology and similarly bridged two disciplines.

This chapter has chronicled how the body of social movement research grew to maturity and became an established and major subfield in the disciplines of both sociology and political science. This was accomplished by shifting the focus of study from the bizarre and irrational to the normal and political. This change, however, begins another story, this time a contemporary one that continues to unfold to this day. One way of characterizing this new narrative is: if we ask the question – as this book does – "What is a social movement?," does the complete and inevitable answer come back as *contentious politics* – that is, simply politics by another means? The next chapter traces the field's dominant theoretical contributions in this vein to suggest the response is: "Yes, social movements are mostly about politics, interests, opportunities and power." The one to follow, chapter 4, suggests that the answer is: "Politics? Well, yes, but social movements are not about group interests and power alone." Cultural forces enter the equation too. The former answer tends to limit explanations of social movements to variables residing in the structural–organizational sphere. By bringing cultural factors back in, the analyst gains access to the ideational and performative dimensions, where a lot of very interesting and important social processes occur.

3
What is a Political Movement?

Most contemporary social movements have a strong political dimension. They usually make their claims in the context of the modern national state. Their targets are mostly politicians, policymakers, and government administrators who are in positions to put into force changes that reflect the specific demands and interests of the movement. As such, they can be considered as a unique brand of in-your-face *contentious politics*. Of course, sometimes the targets are not politicians, as with student protests to change curricula (targeting university officials, e.g., Arthur 2011) or currents of change within religious organizations (targeting church officials, e.g., Bruce 2011), but in the twenty-first century the vast majority of protest campaigns and social movements are ultimately aimed at influencing laws, policies, and government officials. These efforts occur at various levels of governance: municipal, state and provincial, national, and – a comparatively new development – the transnational level, such as the global justice movement or anti-land-mine campaigns. Strategies of influence sometimes take secondary routes such as attracting media attention, convincing bystanders, and swaying public opinion, with the assumption that politicians – presuming a degree of democratic responsiveness – will be influenced by shifts in public attitudes. At the extreme, some movements – insurgencies or revolutionary uprisings – seek to bring down and replace entire political systems – in a sense, the ultimate sort of contentious politics. These tend to occur when political elites are unresponsive to reforms, and positions on both sides harden.

The last chapter traced how this contentious, politics-by-another-means perspective helped normalize the field of social movement research by linking it with themes commonly pursued by political scientists: group interests, policy-making, governance, representation, challenges to entrenched power, and so on. One effect of this is to deemphasize the larger sweep of social change processes in favor of research on the mechanics of specific campaigns. A contentious politics perspective requires data on the nuts and bolts of mobilization and countermobilization – say, over Proposition 8 in California, which defined marriage as a union between a man and woman exclusively. Gay rights groups opposed it; coalitions of Republicans, conservative Christians, Mormons, and retiree groups promoted it. Looking at the strategic and organizational decisions by various groups, the mix of institutional and extrainstitutional tactics, the coalitions and coordination of action in the campaign, and how the initiative eventually passed, nicely captures the contentious politics approach, but it begs the larger questions of the sea change regarding public acceptance of homosexuality that has occurred since the turn of the new millennium. This is a shift that rises above the strictly political and rides on cultural currents. Another effect of this approach is that by laying stress on factors such as organizational efficiency, resources, relative strength of contenders, strategic decisions, and channels of official influence, the processes of social definition, interpretation, framing, and collective identity are deemphasized. Both foci embrace important variables in movement mobilization. The point is that, by laying stress on the structural–organizational dimension of analysis, the analyst tends to close off access to the other dimensions. How practitioners of social movement research navigate this dilemma is a thread of discussion that I will weave through this chapter.

Contemporary trends give credence to the contentious politics emphasis. People increasingly seem to rely not only on political parties and elections to make their preferences known, but also on protests, demonstrations, petition campaigns, marches, and organizations that pursue their demands for social change. There is some evidence that the frequency and size of these phenomena are increasing (Soule and Earl 2005; Dodson 2011), perhaps a reflection of the diversity of interests in modern society, its rapid pace of change, and impatience with the unresponsiveness of elected officials. Because modern polities are complex, claims and grievances are widespread and there will always be groups with demands that are unmet. This encourages groups to mobilize extrainstitutionally. Moreover, new interests will always arise to pose threats to established ones, creating new arenas of political contention. Also, the occurrence of protests in one region or policy domain can spur copycat protests elsewhere, creating the diffusion of protest that can lead to a *protest cycle*, as in the 1960s. For all these reasons, it makes sense to consider how characteristics of politics and governance influence the occurrence of social movements. Another way of putting this is that the *structure of political opportunities*, both for citizen inputs and for the formation of social movements, is fundamental to understanding modern contentious politics.

Structures of Political Opportunity

The concept of political opportunity was introduced during the field's critical mass period. Peter Eisinger (1973) was a political scientist who analyzed the causes of the urban riots that occurred in the US during the 1960s. He looked at cities where riots were intense and compared them with cities where riots did not occur or were relatively mild. He found that variations in the accessibility of political participation in the municipal governments explained why high levels of protest occurred in some cities and lower levels in others, but the relationship was not straightforward. Protest levels were lower where access was more open and also low where it was closed. In between – that is, in the cities with mixed records of openness – protest levels were the highest. The generalizable point seems to be that very open political access decreases protest activity, but mixed and inconsistent accessibility increases it. The social psychology behind these relationships is not anger, frustration, or aggression, but rather the cool calculation of interests and opportunities. When political channels are quite open, activists choose to avoid risks of being jailed, injured, or losing time at work while also calculating a good probability of success by exercising political influence. At the closed end of the spectrum, aggrieved groups see no opportunities for change at all and do not pursue mobilization because the pay-offs are too low. All the action occurs at the intermediate levels because costs of extrainstitutional protest are not too high, and the availability of some opportunities through the established political channels raise the likelihood of success.

Eisinger's findings became fundamental in the political approach to social movements – and remain so to this day. Another key study in the political approach to social movements was Doug McAdam's *Political Process and the Development of Black Insurgency, 1930–1970* (1999 [1982]). His research focused on the African-American civil rights movement, which began in the American South where, in the 1950s, local politics were firmly in the hands of segregationists and few opportunities existed for black political participation. The question McAdam asked was, under these circumstances, why did the civil rights movement begin to mobilize when it did? McAdam's answer traced broad historical changes in the American South's economy and in different levels of government where opportunities might occur – municipal, county, state, and federal in the US. This multi-tiered quality of modern governance is just one of several dimensions that produce a highly complex picture of political opportunities, such that simply saying that they are open or closed glosses several key factors and how they interact.

1   Levels of governance. At all levels, there was little support for black demands prior to the 1950s, although some protests had occurred in the South during the late 1940s. Yet, as the movement's momentum grew during the early to mid-1960s, McAdam notes that issues of public disorder, civil unrest, and school desegregation forced politicians at the federal level to take note. Among individual legislators, support for racial integration was generally limited because of the lack of black electoral influence. Despite popular notions that the Kennedy administration

supported black civil rights, McAdam notes that it was much more concerned with limiting disruptive protests. The Voter Education Project (1962–4) was a politically astute strategy the administration used to channel the movement away from civil disruption while at the same time attracting black voter support in Southern states. McAdam notes that this aversion to civil disorder created opportunities for the movement to elicit federal intervention by the mere threat of violent confrontation (1999 [1982]: 172). A simple open–closed polity model fails to capture this complexity, in which protest levels and political openness are in a dynamic and recursive relationship.

2 Judicial administration. Political opportunities are also affected by the courts, where multiple levels of judicial authority have different effects. At the national level, US Supreme Court decisions – most notably, *Brown* v. *Board of Education of Topeka* (1954) – encouraged black mobilization. Going back to the 1930s, there was a discernable shift in Supreme Court responsiveness toward civil rights arguments, a development that McAdam notes led to changed perceptions among black leaders that government support for segregation may be decreasing (1999 [1982]: 108). There was no such responsiveness evident in the local courts in the American South, however, which remained staunchly segregationist. Courts are also responsible for the enforcement of laws made by the different levels of governance, and when there is conflict at these levels between the law and its enforcement, they must be adjudicated. Political opportunities can vary according to the ability and the intent of administrators and local officials to enforce policies. This may result from variations in public opinion according to geographical region, to which politicians, policy administrators, and law enforcement officers must be responsive if they are to keep their jobs.

3 Political parties. McAdam also noted the effect of the organization of national political parties and how allegiances change according to national policy arenas and a party's candidates. Going back to Reconstruction, Southern whites vilified the Republican Party, the party of

Lincoln, and were solidly Democratic. Southern Democrats were staunchly segregationist and, between 1900
and 1930, repressed black voters in the South and
enforced their subordination. But this was a different
Democratic Party than existed in the North, which
slowly attracted Northern blacks because of Roosevelt's
New Deal policies. In the 1960s, Kennedy's tentative
embrace of the civil rights movement drove Southern
Democrats to the Republican Party while attracting
blacks (McAdam 1999 [1982]: 158).

Comparative studies on political opportunities, especially research focusing on European states, have identified several other party-related factors based on variations
in electoral systems. In countries with parliamentary
systems, opportunities for political participation are more
open because there are more political parties competing
for parliamentary seats. In contrast to the two-party
system of the US, more parties mean more responsiveness
to voter opinion, at least in theory. Responsiveness is
further institutionalized by a common result in parliamentary systems: that no one party receives a voting majority.
The need to form governing coalitions provides access to
the halls of power for minority parties, creating opportunities for movements that have the ear of minority-party
officials. Greater potential for elite divisions and conflicts
also offer more possibilities for social movements to
recruit political allies. This is good for movements, and
increases the likelihood of having their demands met, but
it also reduces extrainstitutional protest, mitigates violent
and disruptive tactics, and integrates SMOs into normal
politics. Open systems have a net calming effect on the
polity, reducing civil disorder – a key goal of most political elites whose interests lie in the status quo.

4   Centralization versus decentralization. States can vary on
the degree of centralization of policymaking and administration. Decentralized systems of government, such as
the federal states of the US, Canada, and Germany, offer
greater political openings for participation than centralized systems, such as in France, the Netherlands, or
Sweden (Kitschelt 1986; Kriesi 1995). A similar logic
applies regarding states that accord greater independence

to legislative and judicial branches, in contrast to those that subordinate functions of governance to the executive ministries. Koopmans and Kriesi (1995) found that the decentralized Swiss federal system moderated protest, as one would expect, but it also facilitated movement mobilization by invigorating civil society and multiplying points of political access. In contrast, the relatively closed and centralized system of France restricted perceptions of citizen efficacy. This was translated into decreased levels of mobilization, but – an important finding – it also tended to radicalize protest campaigns. Perceptions of government unresponsiveness meant that more radical protest strategies were used to get the government's attention.

Opportunities and Threats in Nondemocracies

The studies I have cited so far have been of Western democracies, but it is important to recognize that none of them are *perfectly* open and responsive. There are variations in the democratic character of all "democratic" states – for example Sweden and Norway are commonly seen as more open and responsive than the US or UK. But if we move beyond Western Europe and North America, an even wider range of variation in political opportunities and threats becomes apparent. In general, it is safe to say that political elites everywhere resist challenges to their rule, but the question becomes whether they do so within the law, abiding by the rules of the game, or repress their opponents indiscriminately. Communist party elites in China were mostly unanimous about crushing student prodemocracy protests in Tiananmen Square in 1989. They saw any pressure to increase democratic participation as a significant challenge to their power. China, both then and now, would be considered a relatively repressive autocratic regime with limited political opportunity structures.

Scholars have classified repressive states in terms of their prevailing strategies of political control, size of repressive apparatus, and openness – or lack thereof (Koopmans and Kriesi 1995). At the pole of extreme and overwhelming repressiveness, we find *totalitarian* states. These are often characterized by Orwellian penetration of the state into realms of private life and civil society, ongoing monitoring and social control through a highly developed and extensive police apparatus, strong ideological socialization, and continual propagandizing. Totalitarian states often employ *state terror* to limit opposition. Extensive and arbitrary arrests and executions quash ideological or policy disagreement within the ruling party, and instill fear among citizens. High-capacity totalitarian states (sometimes called Stalinist states) are relatively rare today: North Korea, Belarus, and Tajikistan are examples.

More common are *authoritarian* states, which offer more areas of freedom, usually because they seek to foster a degree of legitimacy among the citizens to facilitate governance but also control dissent. Contemporary China is a good example. It is a one-party state in which the military plays an important role in society and politics. It is not a competitive, multiparty democracy – rather, one party, the Chinese Communist Party, dominates state and society. Other examples of authoritarian states are Mexico before 1988, dominated by the PRI (Partido Revolucionario Institucional), the Eastern European communist countries before 1991, and Mubarak's Egypt before the 2011 revolution. While not open democracies, in these states small spaces of political debate existed (within bounds) among ruling-party members. There were a handful of window-dressing parties with a few seats in the rubber-stamp legislatures. These states have been called "façade democracies," or "party authoritarianisms," many of which are based on networks of local party and union leaders who deliver the vote by distributing favors to their constituents – especially employment – in return for support. Differences of opinion in government agencies may exist, for example, when leaders rely on economic experts to guide modernization policies. These kinds of authoritarian states tend to be quite stable (Geddes 1999).

Yet, controlling all aspects of social life is an impossible task, requiring resource levels and penetration into society that are beyond the capacity of most authoritarian states. This means that authoritarian regimes are riddled with *free spaces* – areas outside state control and surveillance – which serve as opportunities for dissent and criticism (Johnston 2006, 2011). For example, the communist regime in Poland was unable to co-opt the popularity of the Catholic Church. In turn, the church was a major incubator for the mass-based opposition movement called Solidarity that challenged the regime in the early 1980s. Free spaces can play a key role in the development of the opposition because, paradoxically, they give to participants small glimpses of what is possible in a more open society. The paradox is because, far from being unrestrained opportunities for political debate, free spaces are typically secretive and carefully guarded by participants, but there is freedom in the sense of being able to speak one's mind, even if in a constricted way. Free spaces are islands of freedom that serve as training grounds for opposition leaders and wellsprings of early-riser movements.

This is an area I have been interested in for a long time, partly because of the heroic risks some people take for political freedom. Personally, I have always wondered where I would stand if I risked getting jailed or losing my job because of what I taught. This happened to one professor and democratic activist in the USSR whom I interviewed. He was stripped of his university position and sent to work on a chicken farm cleaning pens – a "chicken-shit job," literally – for his outspoken views. In the course of my research in authoritarian regimes such as the old Soviet Union, Eastern Europe, and Francoist Spain (Johnston 1991, 2006), I have learned never to underestimate people's potential for taking risks and finding opportunities – sometimes making their own opportunities – in the most repressive situations.

Political Opportunities, Real and Imagined

W. I. Thomas, an early sociologist, once said, "If people define things as real, they are real in their consequences." Thomas's famous dictum applies to the above examples of protests in closed political systems because people have defined their own opportunities for collective action, despite the risks. In the lingo of social movement theory, what we have here is that political opportunities are *framed* so that action is likely (Gamson and Meyer 1996). It has been observed that movement leaders commonly inflate prospects of success and underestimate obstacles. Insofar as members accept their spin, an opportunity is a matter of seeing it as such. The presumption of much of our discussion so far has been that state structures that facilitate or threaten movement mobilization are perceived straightforwardly, that the "signals" sent and received are not problematic in terms of their interpretation. However, as I found in my own research, there are people who downplay the threats posed by authoritarian states. Following Thomas's dictum, human beings seem to have innate capacity to define some situations in truly fantastic and unreal terms and act upon them accordingly – as in North Korea in late 2009, when citizens protested currency devaluations as if they could actually influence their leaders (Li-sun 2009; McNeill 2009).

Perception of political opportunities mostly rides on social-psychological and cultural processes. An emphasis on these processes stands in contrast to structural analyses that assume that perception of interests and threats presented by the state are, for the most part, not problematic and can be analytically treated as such. In this view, discerning a threat or an advantageous opening is a matter of objective perception and calculation of costs and benefits. This makes deciding to participate in a protest a function of weighing what you get against what you pay, like most economic decisions, and means that these assessments are superficially apparent and unproblematic in terms of interpretation. This logic marks a division between different research approaches to social movements.

As in the preceding chapter, permit me again to draw the contrast starkly in order to identify the underlying issue. There are some researchers who emphasize structural factors – relatively fixed, sometimes institutional relations – among social actors. This emphasis directs their analytical attention to historic configurations of social, political, and economic relations. The interests and threats contained therein are taken to be mostly apparent to acting groups and their members, deemed to be less matters of framing or interpretation than constraints and forced choices. In the world of structural analysis, structure compels action most of the time in the same way. Then, there are some researchers who emphasize cultural processes, who presume that the opportunities presented by large state structures are always collectively interpreted, so that the resulting action is not a *fait accompli*. In this view, to understand protest mobilization, the analyst must delve into collective processes of meaning making, culture, and interpretation. To do this systematically, thoroughly, and accurately is an intensive analytical process of a different sort from in the first perspective. This in part widens the fault line because it means that culturalists expend a lot of effort looking at different data sources than structuralists. From the other side of the fault line, structuralists would tend to see these efforts as diversions from the underlying explanations of why protest movements and revolutions really occur.

In the broad topography of the field of research today, most scholars would agree that a complete analysis of social movement mobilization requires some mix of elements focusing on perception/interpretation (and a commitment to appropriate methodological strategies), as well as those elements that capture "hard" institutional arrangements (and related research methods). While some opportunities and threats compel or constrain action straightforwardly, others do not, and different stages in the mobilization process and different research foci give rise to different mixes – to be settled by painstaking, on-the-ground, empirical research. Reconciliation between structural and interpretative–cultural perspectives has been the keystone of *political process theory*, a synthetic approach that has been widely employed and elaborated by researchers since the mid-1980s, although a fair assessment is that the synthesis is somewhat lopsided in favor of the structural–organizational dimension.

Political Process Theory

Doug McAdam first codified political process theory in his classic study of the rise and decline of the civil rights movement (1999 [1982]). Since then, there have been additions and modifications, most notably the addition of Tilly's (1986) concept of repertoires of contention and the idea of *collective action framing* (Snow, Worden, Rochford, and Benford 1986). It is fair to say that political process theory is the lingua franca among researchers working in politically focused approaches to social movements, but it also provides a little room for elements of interpretative and cultural processes and a basic view of culture. Figure 3.1 distills a huge body of research into its fundamental components, as represented by the four main, unshaded boxes on the left. The endpoint is contentious political mobilization, the fifth box on the right. The model allows that SMOs sometimes pursue a mix of institutional and noninstitutional strategies. The bold arrow at the bottom of the figure sweeps directly to the contentious mobilization box and avoids the middle components. The progression of causal influence moves from various elements of political structure and context on the left side to movement mobilization on the right side, with three key constitutive elements in the middle exerting variable influence depending on the movement being studied. It is fair to say that these middle factors, taken together, represent fundamental research foci for scholars guided by the political process model.

To begin, there are two shaded boxes that lie behind the main elements of the political process model. They are present in the graphic because political process approaches almost always assume two fundamental and general social forces that lie behind the concrete causal elements. First, on the left, behind the box of political opportunities and/or threats, we identify the role of broad social changes. At the most basic level, these are taken to be the starting mechanisms of the mobilization process, and reflect a macrosociological and structural orientation that is present in many applications of political process theory. While these may seem far removed from the movement itself – such as fundamental economic restructuring, the demise of old industries or shifts to global production, changes in the international balance of power or warmaking technologies – their causal influence enters the equation because of how they give rise to new interests or threats to old ones. The second box represents the influences that shifts in public opinion and predominant cultural discourses can play in mobilization.

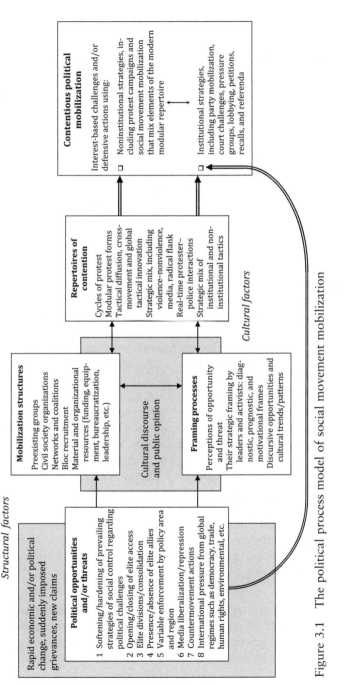

Figure 3.1 The political process model of social movement mobilization

Political opportunities and/or threats

The political opportunities/threats box in the left foreground lists eight basic ways opportunities and threats may arise to spur mobilization. Goldstone and Tilly (2001) have suggested that the state always pairs opportunities with threats, mixing of concessions accorded to some groups and repression of others. Similarly, movement groups weigh the elements in the mix to decide their courses of action. These elements can be subtle, such as hints of granting tax-exempt status to an SMO (an opportunity) or revoking it (a threat), or, more obviously, arresting leaders, which might either spur mobilization or thwart it. Threats are the opposite of opportunities and, when they occur, either by changing state policies or through altered political contexts, they can spur collective action to prevent these changes. Such movements tend to be conservative, reactive, and right-wing. Sometimes they are countermovements to defend threatened interests or statuses. For example, Van Dyke and Soule (2002) observe that right-wing militia groups in the US formed in reaction to political and economic threats arising from loss of employment in manufacturing and farming, and cultural shifts in changing gender roles. Yet, threats by themselves are not usually sufficient for mobilization, and in nondemocratic regimes threat in the form of state repression usually inhibits protest, except when it is disproportionally violent, which sometimes leads to mobilization. This is exactly what happened in the Syrian civil war. It has been suggested that this mix of opportunity and threat should be thought of as the "signals" that are sent to movements, and that the perception of these signals is the key to political opportunity effects (Minkoff and Meyer 2004).

Of the eight items listed in the opportunities/threats box, the six items below represent the broad consensus on influential factors among political-process scholars, building on McAdam's listing (1999 [1982]).

- Prevailing strategies of social control. Some states and/or local levels of governance are democratic and some are not. Some exercise heavy-handed social control via the police and security forces; others do not. Where a political regime falls on the variable of social control is a fundamental element of opportunity/ threat.

- Changes in elite access represent another consensus element. It refers to how a political regime's shift to increase internal points of access for challenging groups can affect mobilization levels. In practice, the effects of this variable are highly dependent on other factors. On the one hand, if greater elite access is superficial or limited, it can increase perceptions that elite resistance is weakening or cracking (see the next bullet point), and that probabilities of success have inched upward. This, in turn, spurs mobilization efforts to intensify through a new interpretation of possibilities. On the other hand, if access to policymaking elites is genuine, the effect may be to decrease protest mobilization because institutional strategies are more direct, effective, and have lower costs. This opportunity dimension highlights a common thread in some political-process approaches: that how opportunities are perceived must be factored into the equation.

- Elite divisions. A common situation in contemporary politics is that elite players jockey for power among themselves. When ruling-elite division is significant, it creates opportunities for political movements by focusing elite attention on internecine battles and palace intrigues. It also fosters the impression that elite opposition to challengers may be fracturing. The variable of elite divisions is relative in the sense that there is always competition for power at the top, even within the most closed and repressive authoritarian regimes, as we saw in the Chinese Communist Party leadership change in 2012, but when competition becomes so intense as to affect social control functions, opportunities for challenges open.

- Elite allies. The above factor raises the possibility that some political elites will turn to outside challengers for support in their quest for power. We discussed how multiparty parliamentary systems offer more opportunities for citizen input. In repressive regimes too, divisions among ruling elites often take the form of hardliners versus reformists. The latter group may open opportunities for challenging groups to increase their public support at local levels and leverage in the ruling party.

- Variable enforcement of policies was discussed as a regional factor of regime structure. In the US, we saw its influence regarding the variable enforcement of voting rights in the segregationist South. Here too, this factor functions in repressive regimes such as China, where much greater latitude is given to citizen organizations and local protests in the southern province of Guangzhou. Similarly, the Chinese state varies its repression of protests by policy arena. After the Sichuan earthquake in 2008, parents who lost their children when schools collapsed took to the streets to protest against shoddy construction. Many of these protests were allowed to take place, but not all of them were, and selective repression was often aimed at leaders. Here we find a good example of the mix of opportunity and threat signals sent by the state.
- Changes in media openness. It is common that social movements "make news by making noise," with the strategic justification that media coverage draws in bystander publics and those who may be favorably disposed but have so far remained inactive. Favorable media coverage can influence public opinion, which, in turn, influences politicians and policymakers. Press freedoms are an important measure of openness. Authoritarian regimes, like China, seek to limit what gets into the news. In 2011, the Chinese Ministry of Propaganda placed tight restrictions on reporting about the Arab Spring. Fearing that reports of street-filled protests for democracy might encourage similar mobilizations in China, internet news and newspapers came under strict surveillance, although news leaked in through Hong Kong and offshore internet providers.

Framing processes

The framing processes box represents one way that the political process model incorporates elements of the ideational–interpretative sphere into the causal equation. Specifically, collective action is embedded in broader cultural discourses that are historically specific. For example, issues of sexual orientation and associated rights were not topics discussed in the public forum at all 100 years ago, nor were there mobilization efforts to voice demands. To move from general cultural trends to concrete collective action, framing theory identifies three basic interpretative processes that must occur (Snow and Benford 1988). First, leaders must develop a *diagnostic frame* that identifies the problem in a way that is meaningful for a critical mass of people. Next, they must arrive at assessments of what is to be done – the *prognostic frame*. This specifies how people should act collectively and defines the contours of the movement. Finally, a *motivational frame* must be developed to help with the mobilization task of getting people into the streets.

Framing is a major perspective in the field of social movement research that emphasizes – as discussed in chapter 1 – the ideational and interpretative elements of movements. It is closely related to the concept of ideology in that systematic ideologies also diagnose problems, make prognoses of what must be done, and give motivation for action. The concept of framing expands McAdam's idea of *cognitive liberation*, which referred to how movement participants must break out of old ways of thinking. Establishing new frames of interpretation is a fundamental process by which people can come to see old injustices in new ways. The presumption in a lot of framing research is that movement leaders and activists, often in strategic planning among themselves, arrive at framings of movement themes and ideas to motivate actions and attract new supporters. Of course, the other side of the coin is that cultural patterns and public opinion also shape how a movement frames its message. Snow and Benford (1992) introduced the concept of *master frames* to capture the influence of broad patterns of values and beliefs held by the public, which influence how specific collective action frames are shaped. Movements that can link their messages to dominant master frames are more likely to be successful (Diani 1996). To defend access to legal abortions in the US, the pro-abortion movement cast its arguments in terms of an "abortion rights frame" that was nested within a larger master frame of citizen rights that grew out of the civil rights movement and the women's movement, both of which used widely recognized and accepted conceptions of civil rights upheld by courts and by the US Constitution.

Repertoires of contention

The development of modern ways of protesting was a historical–cultural process that began in the nineteenth century and, in the twenty-first century, embraces the broad repertoire of actions that are widely shared and understood as appropriate actions – marches, speeches, meetings, sit-ins, strikes, singing, and so on. Repertoires, like framing, are influenced by cultural templates that are shared conceptions of what is right and appropriate, and how to do things.

Within the modern repertoire, movement groups make strategic and tactical choices about how to pursue their goals. But from a crossnational perspective, there is a surprising continuity in the modern repertoire, regardless of national context. The elements of the modern repertoire are modular protest forms that diffuse widely from other movements via cycles of protest (Tarrow 1989). They influence strategic decisions about the mix of nonviolent and violent actions, relations with the media, and relations with other groups, both moderate and extremist (a movement's "radical flank"). However, when protesters take to the streets and confront the police or counterprotesters, it is not uncommon that events take a course that could not have been predicted by all the tactical planning in the world. Thus, the actual playing out of a repertoire is not completely determined by the existing stock of tactics from other movements, but rather is guided by it in important ways – a foundation around which innovations occur. In practice, the received repertoire is constantly being renewed.

Mobilizing structures

The central role of pre-existing organizations is one of the most enduring findings about social movement mobilization. *Mobilizing structures* are "those collective vehicles, informal as well as formal, through which people mobilize and engage in collective action" (McAdam, Tarrow and Tilly 1996). Mobilization structures are based on the groups and associations that constitute civil society and in which people gather every day. They can be of political, class, religious, and/or ethnic character, and because they are already constituted, they are ready-made vehicles through which members defend their interests. Mobilizing structures also partly shape perceptions of opportunity, framing processes, and repertoires of contention, as the direction of the arrows in figure 3.1 depicts. Membership in these pre-existing groups waxes and wanes according to prevailing public opinion, cultural patterns, and trends, as does the degree to which these organizations feed members into SMOs.

McAdam (1999 [1982]) used the term "indigenous organizations" to capture the idea that the civil rights movement grew from organizations already constituted in the black community. The NAACP (National Association for the Advancement of Colored People), CORE (Congress of Racial Equality), and FOR (Fellowship of Reconciliation) worked to further racial equality by exerting political pressure on behalf of black interests. But also there were groups and organizations whose political significance lay in potential yet to be developed. Black colleges throughout the South were small and underfunded prior to roughly 1930, but thereafter they grew rapidly, especially after 1940. This increase was a result of growing financial support from churches, foundations, the United Negro College Fund, and, surprisingly, Southern state governments, which saw black colleges as a way to foster segregation. As far as the civil rights movement was concerned, these colleges throughout the South provided cadres of dedicated activists.

Another mobilizing structure for the civil rights movement was the African-American church in the South. The church was the most extensive and developed associational vehicle for Southern blacks. According to E. Franklin Frazier, "As a result of the elimination of Negroes from the political life . . . the Negro Church became the arena of their political activities." Frazier continues that, for men seeking power and status in the black community, church politics were especially important (Frazier 1963: 43). Morris's study of the organizational origins of the civil rights movement (1984) gives special importance to the place of the church in the early phases of the movement, such as the Montgomery bus boycott, out of which grew the Montgomery Improvement Association, and later the Southern Christian Leadership Conference (SCLC).

The American South was extremely repressive of black civil and political rights, and in other repressive situations we can find early church-based mobilizing structures. In Catalonia and the Basque region (under the authoritarian Francoist regime in Spain), in Lithuania and Ukraine (against the Soviets), and in Poland and Eastern Germany (against the communists), ruling elites permitted churches to exist because they (incorrectly) saw them as safe alternatives to political activities. As in the American South, this created openings that activists were able to exploit (Johnston 1991; Johnston and Mueller 2001). It may be that the same is going on right now in China with respect to its policies regarding rapidly growing Christian churches, especially house churches (Vala and O'Brien 2007; Johnston and Carnesecca 2014). The take-away points are that: (1) while these mobilizing structures are not SMOs per se, and their organizing principles are sometimes apolitical, challenging movements almost always have roots in pre-existing social groupings; (2) by allowing such free spaces to exist, elites create political opportunities for mobilization in ways that they cannot anticipate.

Structure, Culture, and Contentious Politics

It is fair to say that political process theory has provided the main rubric for understanding social movements since the early 1990s. Although during this period there have been debates about the theory's underestimation of cultural and interpretative processes (Goodwin and Jasper 2004) on the one hand, and of rational calculation of costs, benefits, and thresholds on the other (Lichbach 1997), political process concepts have dominated research agendas in the field. One of the reasons for this is the simple fact that almost all movements occur in state systems and seek to influence political outcomes and/or state policymaking (Johnston 2011). Yet the complexity of the model as depicted in figure 3.1 is daunting, and makes one wonder whether social science cannot do better. A widely shared goal of social scientists is to seek the simplest and clearest explanatory models. Because the political process approach has not given "theoretical parsimony" by any stretch of the imagination, it has increasingly been criticized on several dimensions.

First, several observers have noted that the concept of political opportunity is so broad and inclusive that it tells us very little. According to Gamson and Meyer (1996: 275), it risks being a "sponge that soaks up virtually every aspect of the social movement environment . . . an all encompassing fudge factor." Examples of suggested "political opportunities" that stretch the definition include: (1) the shape and popularity of previous movements (Minkoff 1997); (2) the ideological openness of political parties (Amenta and Zylan 1991; Kriesi et al. 1995; Rucht 1996); (3) international alliances, pressures, and regimes (McAdam 1999 [1982]; Smith 2008); and (4) "discursive opportunities" (Koopmans and Statham 1999), referring to conducive cultural trends, ideas, and language.

Second, there is always the risk of tautology when the analyst looks for positive events in a movement's trajectory. The strong tendency is to see them as essential for its success. Is every positive development for a social movement a political opportunity? Also, there is no such a thing as a negative opportunity, which is why it is important to balance the concept by looking for threats as well. Searching for opportunities is mostly after-the-fact analysis that risks diminishing the negative cases that would make the concept verifiable. Moreover, it is hard to identify opportunities before activists take advantage of them. We learn very little that is not self-apparent from the idea that open opportunities are good for protest mobilization and that, when they are absent, negative consequences result.

Third, there is a static quality to the analysis in that the "opportunities" to mobilize presented by the state are relatively fixed structures and apprehended as such by movement participants. Movements interact with the state and with countermovements in a strategic dance (Meyer and Staggenborg 1996). Moreover, movements can create their own opportunities (Casquette 1996; Ramos 2008), as when huge protests cause divisions among elites about how to deal with popular demands. There is no room for this kind of dynamism in figure 3.1. In recent years, this critique has led to a more process-oriented and dynamic approach among some researchers, based on McAdam, Tarrow, and Tilly's (2001) dynamics of contention perspective (see also McAdam and Tarrow 2011). This is a project that comes at social movements from a different angle, seeking to identify general processes and mechanisms that are found in all instances of movement development. For example, regarding mobilizing structures, the task would be to identify the mechanisms by which the membership of a church group gets transformed into an SMO. How this is accomplished, in part, brings in cultural-interpretative processes of group definition, conformity, and boundary enforcement by contending groups – topics for the next chapter. Other basic mechanisms would be how contacts among SMOs are brokered in a movement, or how perceptions of opportunities and threats can intensify and/or diverge.

Fourth, a large body of research stresses the importance of resources in mobilization. Political process theorists, to distinguish themselves from their conceptual forebears in the RM perspective, have thrown the baby out with the bath water, so to speak, by diminishing the role of resources. Presumably resources enter into the equation via the box of mobilizing structures, but these mostly refer to organizational patterns of recruitment and not the determining role of money, organizational acumen, and resources in a movement's success (Ramos 2008; Jasper 2012).

Finally, despite attempts to synthesize structural and interpretative factors, leading scholars such as Goodwin and Jasper (2004) have commented that political process theory's keystone concept – political opportunities – carries biases that obscure cultural, social-psychological, cognitive, and emotional influences. Some researchers have suggested a number of "soft" opportunities based on perception and social construction, such as "discursive opportunity structures" (Koopmans and Statham 1999), but this takes us back to our first criticism about the sponginess of the concept, broadening even more a concept that already is too vague. Might it not be better to step outside the political process framework to better understand where the processes of social construction are fully relevant?

This is precisely what I do in the next chapter on "cultural movements." There I discuss movements in which Thomas's dictum – "If people define things as real, they are real in their consequences" – takes a primary place. In this chapter, however, Marx's 18th Brumaire dictum takes precedence: "Men [and women] make their own history, but they do not make it just as they please." Political structures shape mobilization in important ways for many types of social movements, constraining human agency and choices, but not for all movements in strictly determining ways.

4
What is a Cultural Movement?

In this chapter I will navigate the murky waters of culture and politics. Why murky? They are partly so because of the pervasive nature of culture. Simply stated, there is nothing outside of culture. No given social grouping, social institution, or SMO can have more or less culture because they are thoroughly and entirely cultural (Norton 2004: 2). Also, culture is in a continual process of becoming. Our actions not only reflect culture, they also reaffirm it and create it anew. This makes cultural influences especially difficult to measure and to trace systematically. To compound matters, social movements have their own cultures that are embedded in the broader culture, drawing on parts of it, challenging or rejecting other parts, and changing it in small ways by their own actions. Finally, the waters are murky because of the synergy between culture and politics: political Islam, contention over gay marriage or abortion, and the constant intrusion of religion into political discourse, especially in the US. This last point raises the question of the relationship between cultural factors and interest-based contention about power and influence.

There is no doubt that some movements are driven by stark conflicts of interests between the challengers and their targets. Others, however, place emphasis on identity, community, and proxy causes such as animal rights or anti-whaling campaigns, where interests seem distant from protagonists' daily lives. It is entirely plausible that research about some movements that lie mostly in the realm of contentious politics needs the tools of cultural analysis *to a lesser degree*. To put it differently, to the extent that interests, political power, and structure are more central in a social movement's coalescence and mobilization, these factors seem to constrain it more, rendering its ideologies, interpretative processes, and cultural artifacts relatively less open-ended, less subject to process-based analyses, and therefore less central in the causal equation – but never *completely unnecessary*, I would venture to say. The other side of the coin is the focus of this chapter – that is, there are some movements for which cultural processes of working through ideas and identities are central.

Great care is needed here, and the consequences for our understanding of social movements are significant. When interests seem to be very clear and unambiguous, the danger is that of relegating cultural processes to stepchild status, which risks closing off alternative explanations too quickly. For example, political process explanations were widely accepted for the Montgomery bus boycott in 1954–5. Scholars recognize the boycott as the spark of the black civil rights movement in the US, and interest-based and opportunity-based explanations, such as structural shifts after World War II and the changing political opportunities of the period, have been widely applied to it. But Shultziner (2013) argues convincingly that on-the-ground shared experiences and emergent definitions of insult and unfairness among bus users in Montgomery, and not broad structural changes, were the primary causes of the boycott. He presents strong evidence that, just prior to the boycott, collective experiences of humiliation and shame increased sharply on the buses, and that looking closely at what blacks were saying about this in 1954 points clearly to why the boycott occurred when it did. The point is that tendencies to focus on political opportunity interpretations meant that important countervailing data about interaction and interpretation were missed.

My strategy here is to consider movements with a strong cultural emphasis to balance a focus on interests, opportunities, and threats. Although cultural themes have been visible from time to time among researchers (Johnston and Klandermans 1992; Johnston 2009), they are mostly woven in the background of the field. In the past decade, however, there are indications that this may be changing. There has been a revival of research interest in the collective experience and social construction of emotions, in new approaches to framing, in performance aspects of mobilization, and in narrative and textual approaches (Johnston 2009). There is also a revival of interest in dynamic and process-oriented elements of contentious politics (McAdam, Tarrow, and Tilly 2001; McAdam and Tarrow 2011), which, although not culturalist per se, emphasize the generalizable processes and mechanisms of movement development and invariably bring to the analysis elements of social construction, interaction, and collective definitions. These are disparate strands, to be sure, but they all center on the intersection of the ideational–interpretative and performative spheres of analysis from chapter 1 and shift the field away from an exclusive structural–organizational focus.

Social Movement Culture

Social movement researchers have long recognized that cultural artifacts play important roles in mobilization processes. The artifact concept refers to concrete, often-material, cultural productions, such as the "high-cultural" artifacts of music, poetry, literature, theatre, opera, the plastic arts. Nineteenth-century movements of nationalism often gave rise to music and literature that inspired movements of political independence. Today, there are counterparts in popular culture: rhymes, graffiti, folksongs, logos, popular music, iconic images such as Che and Guy Fawkes. The songs of the civil rights movement and the labor movement (Eyerman and Jamison 1998; Rosigno and Danaher 2004; Rosenthal and Flacks 2012) were important components in mobilizing people to action. The strong and chiseled images of working-class heroes on socialist and communist posters, the ubiquitous graffiti of the South American Left, the lines of poetry that challenged the Soviet censorship (and often landed poets in jail) are strongly symbolic elements of social movements. They represent the ideologies and injustices that animate their production, and the collective action frames that develop as others come to share in their interpretations. These elements can generate strong emotions, and inspire and reflect themes of injustice and struggle. One of the important insights that cultural sociology can offer protest studies is that such artifacts have key roles in social movement mobilization. They can take on "life of their own" because they often carry a prescribed range of appropriate responses (Latour 1987). In varying degrees, artifacts also require the active complicity of an audience to engage their meanings. Because artifacts often have a material quality, it is easy to lose sight of the basic fact that their mobilizing power derives from how they are interpreted by audiences.

Art as artifact

It is fair to say that, for most social movement researchers, high-cultural and/or pop-cultural artifacts do not occupy central concerns, but most would recognize that music can be an especially potent motivator, and is probably the most widely studied. Music has been a factor in many major movements, such as the labor movement, the civil rights movement, socialism in Chile, various ethnonationalist movements, and the anarchist punk scene (Denisoff and Peterson 1973; Halker 1991; Eyerman and Jamison 1998; Rosigno and Danaher 2004; Rosenthal and Flacks 2012). Indeed, there are some movements in which songs, anthems, and the symbolic stature of a musician or a musical group are so important that seeing music as *just* an artifact – that is, once removed from the real causal forces – or *just* a resource to build solidarity, misses the point. Following Rosenthal and Flacks (2012), music not only can function to build collective identity, or to pass information, or preserve a tradition, but also can be integral in the unfolding performance of the movement itself. Music and songs are given significance by participants that can foster solidarity and emotionalize resistance. The significance of music can also be shaped by the movement's opponents.

In the Czechoslovak democracy movement (1968–89) the songs by the rock band Plastic People of the Universe had special resonance among young people. In the immediate post-Prague-Spring period, when the movement was reeling from defeat after the Russian invasion, the band was embraced as a symbol of resistance. This was curious, because during the band's career, which spanned 20 years, only one song in their repertoire might be considered overtly political. The band's political power came from its audience, and how it perceived the state's reaction to the band. The hard-line communist regime in Czechoslovakia saw the band as dangerous, thereby giving it an oppositional significance that band members did not seek. In the words of the band's manager, "We were just a band of freaks, playing rock and roll. . . . It was the problem of the communist government and the party that they didn't like us. They didn't like our aesthetics because it was something from the West – longhairs, capitalism" (quoted in Pareles 2007). Vaclav Havel, playwright, dissident activist, and later president of Czechoslovakia, supported the band, and one of its albums was recorded at his farm. It is plausible that, without the state's drawing attention to it, the band would have faded away as but a footnote to Czech popular culture, but its politicization stresses the importance of the audience, which included here both the public and the state. Dissidents, students and young people, police agents, and communist party members all attributed meanings to the music so that it became iconic of the opposition.

When repression is heavy, artistic production often constitutes a central element of the *oppositional culture*, especially in early stages of movement development. Its central role is largely, first, because creativity and artistic freedoms are so much at odds with authoritarian control; and, second, because ambiguity of the message and popularity of the artists means they are often hard to repress (Johnston and Mueller 2001). Czech theatres, for example, were also identified with the opposition via linkages with the dissident community. Theatres were focal points for organizing the Civic Forum, the main dissident group that authored Charter 77 (Goldfarb 1980). Plays used oppositional language that was "clear to sympathetic spectators but unintelligible to the totalitarian watchdogs of culture" (Oslzly 1990: 99). Especially among ethnic nationalist movements, such as in Quebec, Catalonia, the Basque region, Armenia, and Georgia (under the USSR), high culture and popular-culture elements often embodied political aspirations that found little sympathy among political elites. This was evident in the songs of Gilles Vigneault, Claude Léveillée and the other *chansonniers* (Quebec), Raimón and Lluis Llach (leaders of the *nova cançó* in Catalonia), and the nationalist punk music of Negu Gorriak (Basque region).

Yet it is important to be clear: even when repression is lighter and political opportunities more open, there are cases when aspects of *movement culture* – and primary among these are its musical, graphic, and performative artifacts – play key roles in the movement's organization and mobilization. When a movement's interests and claims are less clear and direct, and when movement goals, identity, and solidarity are complex, analyzing its artifactual symbolism can be helpful in understanding the motivations and interpretations of participants. For example, the punk movement is broadly antiestablishment, highly diverse, but not specific as to its motivating interests. It accords music, dress, and performative self-presentation focal roles in the way it develops its narratives of antiracism, anarchism, rebellion, and community (Moore and Roberts 2009; Haenfler 2006; Duncombe 1997). In contrast, for movements where interests are clear and demands concrete – in the woman suffrage movement of the nineteenth century or the contemporary landless workers movement in Brazil – art and music are not at the forefront. Not that they are absent or inappropriate research topics, but they are more like icing on the cake when considering the main forces that mobilize participants. The mix, ultimately, is an empirical question to be settled by research.

Text as artifact

When repression eases or in countries where it is less obtrusive, the symbolism of music and art becomes less important. A movement's artifactual production can shift to textual forms because language is better adapted to representing complex ideas. Like music, theatre, and art, the linguistic production of a movement – its texts and discourse – are also powerful artifacts that have lives long after their initial production and offer the analyst access to the meanings attributed by participants. It is fairly recently that the social sciences have come to recognize the importance of written and spoken texts as more than just vehicles of ideas, and recognition has been especially slow to reach the study of social movements. Among the early research, Wuthnow (1989) looked at the texts of the Reformation, the Enlightenment, and European socialism to trace the broad contours of discursive communities. Johnston (1991), in contrast, took a microscopic approach by analyzing the movement discourse – both stories and tracts – from linguistically informed perspectives. In between, there are middle-range approaches that look at the organization's production of texts as narratives and stories that have structures of their own (Polletta 2006a, 2009). In all cases, the artifactual element was captured by focusing on representative texts, such as Luther's writings for the Reformation, widely distributed calls for protest at key junctures of the movement (Johnston and Alimi 2013), or documents that capture a key movement issue – for example, Steinberg's (1999: 114–17) close analysis of the Wages Protection Act.

Used in these ways, texts give insight into the shape of a group's communicative behaviors, or its discourse. Discourse, simply stated, is what is said in a group, how it's said, and how it's interpreted. While it is diverse and multifaceted, it is also the connective tissue of a group's collective existence. In this broad sense, the totality of a group's words and meanings can itself be understood as a text performed by the participants. Cultural theorists sometimes point to the interconnectedness of all symbolic action within a group, and how it is "read" by participants. This is an approach that portrays the entirety of a group's culture as a "text" or "discourse" (Norton 2004: 22; Alexander and Mast 2006: 15). At the broadest macrolevel, there are world-historical discourses (*mentalités*, *Zeitgeist*) such as the Enlightenment, Islamism, nineteenth-century liberalism, and 21st-century neoliberalism, which have complex layers and internal dynamics of their own. These are broad discourses (or *discursive fields*) that influence and shape movement-specific discourses, such as feminism, liberation theology, or ecology. Rochon (1998) points out that the movement level often reflects these broad discursive elements that resonate among the larger populace.

In practical terms, discursive analysis usually takes more concrete objects as its focus of study: pamphlets, manifestos, minutes or recollections of meetings and strategy sessions, slogans, speeches, media coverage, public statements of leaders, organizational records, actions of political demonstrators – in other words, the written and spoken text of a movement. When a movement is structured according to different SMOs, the textual production of each forms part of the movement's multivocal discourse, typically reflecting the conflicts, struggles, and political divisions of the broader social and cultural environment. Discursive analysts often use the plural form, *discourses*, to emphasize that what is being discussed and acted upon is never unanimous, but frequently challenged and negated by opposing groups. Contemporary discursive perspectives also stress the emergent and agentic character of textual production, variably called the discursive/rhetorical approach (Billig 1992, 1995), the rhetorical turn (Simon 1990), or the dialogic perspective (Steinberg 1999). These approaches stress that all meaning is strongly context-specific, multifaceted, ever-evolving, and contested.

An important textual focus that has recently emerged among social movement researchers looks at stories or narratives (the terms are interchangeable) that participants and activists tell. Narrative analysis is a subdimension of a broad discursive approach, and often focuses on the compelling stories of injustice or decisions to stand up and be heard (Polletta 2006a, 2009). Other times, analysts look at the powerful stories that are appropriated by movements to be told and retold as ways to spark new interpretations of social relations and spur action. For example, in the late 1970s, the Sandinista opposition to the Somoza regime in Nicaragua drew upon the story of Augusto Sandino's struggle against US military occupation decades earlier. Sandino's death at the hands of Somoza's father gave the story an even more compelling quality. Similarly, the Zapatista uprising in Chiapas, Mexico, in 1994 drew upon the iconography of Emiliano Zapata, the Mexican revolutionary (Jansen 2007). Selbin (2010) notes that the use of similarly powerful stories is a frequent element of insurgencies, revolutions, and ethnic–national rebellions that is often overlooked by analysts working in structuralist perspectives. Their mobilizing role should not be discounted, even in these large-scale structurally based challenges.

Narratives are especially powerful because everyone knows a good story when they hear one. Stories set the scene, lay out the actions, build tensions to a climax and then wrap it all up with a moral evaluation. They also gain their power by leaving certain elements unstated or ambiguous, which draws the audience into the storytelling act to fill in the blanks. To quote Francesca Polletta, a key researcher in social movement narratives: "To study narratives sociologically, then, is to study not only stories but also stories' performance" (2009: 38). Social scientists in linguistics and anthropology have long recognized that there is something primordial and compelling about telling stories. It is common, then, that dominant institutions also have narratives that reflect their undergirding logics and assumptions. They also draw parallels with other well-known stories of a culture, imparting to status-quo relations a natural quality and excluding other possibilities of action, which subtly limits the range of challenges. Insofar as movements contend with existing power relations, they must offer narratives that overcome these constraints of dominant narrative. The bottom line is that good stories can do this, which is why social movement researchers accord them importance. They are rhetorical tools that can be highly persuasive in bringing in new participants, in creating new identities, in building solidarity, and in withstanding adversity and loss (Voss 1998).

Cultural Movements

Romanticism was a broad intellectual, literary, and artistic trend of the nineteenth century with wide ramifications in the social thought and "high culture" of the period – music, poetry, and visual arts. Arising as an intellectual reaction to changes wrought by the industrial revolution and the rationalization of life, Romanticism stressed nature, emotions, artistic experience, heroism, and creativity. On the one hand, it shared some characteristics with social movements. There were clear spaces where it was organized – say, Oxford and Heidelberg Universities – which were centers of Romantic poetry. There were networks of various visual artists and literary salons in various European capitals that gave the movement a structural foundation. There were ideological leaders, and resource issues concerning the support of its practitioners and venues for their works. Finally, there were clear effects in the political realm – for example, in the form of Romantic nationalism – but this was a secondary offspring of its ideological musings and creative activities. On the other hand, Romanticism stands apart from the movements of the previous chapter: its strong ideational and creative focus, its lack of straightforward correspondence with collective interests, and a performance repertoire that resided outside the modern one. There were no demonstrations or marches advocating Romanticism.

Closer to contemporary times, the hippie movement of the 1960s might too be labeled a cultural movement for the same reasons. Although it was certainly less highbrow than Romanticism with its focus on sex, drugs, rock-and-roll, and rebellious exuberance, it too had long-term ramifications in popular culture – in individualism, informality, fashion, entertainment, new-age beliefs, and sexual mores. While it was not an intellectual movement in the strictest sense, and lacked any strategic planning or formal organizations, it did have its discourses, ideologies, and ideologues (Ken Kelsey, Timothy Leary, Alan Cohen, and Alan Ginsburg). Other movement characteristics were present too, for example its central network nodes, like the Diggers, Drop City, The Farm, and spaces for collective identity formation, such as the numerous communes that were stop-overs for itinerant hippies, and the regular gatherings, "be-ins," and concerts (Bill Graham, Stewart Brand), which were platforms for cultural performances of the movement. Various underground newspapers were the media of the movement, such as the *East*

Village Other, the *Berkeley Barb*, and the *Los Angeles Free Press*. In its purest form, the hippie movement eschewed politics, but soon sectors became involved in antiwar protests, and, through confrontations with police – such as the Peoples Park incident in 1969 and Resurrection City – the cultural elements of the hippies broached political action, most notably in the actions of the Yippies.

These examples evince a mix of some characteristics typical of the social movements discussed in the last chapter, but they also tend to lay emphasis on elements that stand apart. First, there is the lack of a clear political focus at their core, which means that concepts such as mobilizing structures, channels of political access, the state, and social control are less relevant (but not *irrelevant*). Second – and closely related to the first point – they are not clear reflections of collective interests, pressing injustices, and/or immediate demands in the way that the US civil rights movement of the 1960s was, or the antiauthoritarian movements of the Arab Spring of 2011. Third, there is a relatively greater emphasis on the ideations, artifacts, and performance aspects of mobilization, such as music, dress, and shared experiences. This means a deemphasis on elements of the standard social movement repertoire: marches, demonstrations, speeches, and protest rallies. Fourth, there is relatively greater influence on how these "movements" work through public opinion or attitudes instead of legislation or policy change. They are strongly defined as movements of ideas and performance rather than interests and politics. Despite these differences, these movements are highly deserving of social science analysis because of the profound and long-lasting impacts they have on society.

Religious Movements

The spiritual dimension of religious movements means that, in their purest form, they eschew issues of collective interests, economics, and power. Placing aside the readers' beliefs about things unseen, for social scientists this means that religious movements are mostly based on social construction, interpretation, and cultural performance. It also may imply that their movement cultures – the ritual performances, beliefs, norms, identities, and dogmas that guide member behaviors – have a more prominent role in their organization, more so than for issue-focused or interest-driven social movements.

Religious movements – or sectarian movements, as they are sometimes called – have as their core organizing principles spiritual matters, theology, and conversion of unbelievers. They often gather momentum, organize, recruit new members, plan and strategize, and run up against resistance, just as their worldly social movement cousins do. However, religious movements mostly coalesce around interpretations of scriptures, words of prophets or gurus, and spiritual concerns, and not collective claims, grievances, and demands whose roots lie in social structure and measurable inequalities. When religious movements organize and pursue resources in the worldly realm – which, to persist, all must eventually do – then their otherworldly and spiritual concerns begin to take a backseat, and their similarities with social movements come to the foreground. That is when their activities become the subject matter of social movement researchers, as when local Mormon wards in my neighborhood promoted the California anti-gay-marriage initiative, Proposition 8.

Mormonism began in the US as a small religious cult of believers in the early nineteenth century. It grew under the leadership of Joseph Smith, who claimed to have received prophecies that became the basis of the new faith. By all accounts, his early followers – his circle of friends and acquaintances – were swept up by religious fervor and dedication, but also were confronted with suspicion and persecution by their neighbors, for whom Smith's teachings were both crazy and heretical. Mormonism, as it gained momentum in the nineteenth century, was a religious movement in the full sense of the term.

Yet, out of these purely spiritual concerns, the group soon broached the political realm regarding the early Mormon practice of polygamy. For Mormons, it was a matter of dogma, but neighbors found it objectionable and enforced civic ordinances against it. Later, when Mormons moved westward to defend their beliefs, escape persecution, and lay claim to their North American "New Jerusalem," political issues regarding governance of a new, religious minority group and their Constitutional rights became issues that had to be confronted, again politically. The point is that while Mormonism was primarily a religious movement, it could scarcely avoid politics. Today, it would be incorrect to label Mormonism a "movement" because of its size and institutionalization. Like many successful social movements, it has become part of the social landscape in less controversial and contentious ways, yet its beliefs still motivate participation in politics, as in its opposition to gay marriage or support for Mitt Romney's presidential campaign in 2012.

The case of Mormonism demonstrates that there are movement characteristics in exclusively religious organizations, especially internal issues relating to recruitment, organization, bureaucratization, social control, commitment, social constructionism, and framing. Religious sects typically begin small when they first split from main churches, but the ones that grow develop a network structure – of communities and centers of worship – typical of social movements. Sectarian splits usually develop over interpretations of dogma, which parallel ideological battles that are common in social movement networks. Also, when religious organizations grow, they risk diluting religious teachings and spiritual fervor, dilemmas that parallel challenges faced by political parties and large SMOs in the era of professionalization (Michels 1962 [1911]; Zald and Ash 1966; McCarthy and Zald 1973). Finally, for many people, their faith goes to the heart of their life-world and identity, which reflects identity-construction processes in many contemporary movements. These parallels suggest that, although not about collective interests or social change, religious movements share many processes with social movements.

The secularization of Western culture has meant the decreasing relevance of religion in society and, as a consequence, decreasing interest among scholars. One review found only a single chapter about religious movements in major books about social movements (Kniss and Burns 2004). My guess is that this is not going to change, but it may be that secularization inappropriately diverts research attention from important questions that religious movements can shed light on, and unintentionally closes off potential sources of data and insight.

New Social Movements

The term *new social movements* carries an implicit contrast
with "old social movements." Old social movements are
those that reflect a strong conflict of interests, especially interests that intersect with major structural divisions in society.
The best example is the labor movement, where conflict with
owners over wages, safety, benefits, and working conditions
is fundamental for its working-class members. Moreover,
workers spend eight hours a day engaged in these issues. The
demands that they fight for relate to their livelihoods and
support for families. The term *new social movements* (here-
after, simply NSMs) was introduced by European researchers
as they recognized that more and more movements occurred
outside of this class-cleavage model. These were movements
about themes such as the environment, women's rights,
animal rights, antiestablishment and countercultural lifestyles, students' rights, and gay rights. These are issues important to their members, but – as the theory goes – not in the
starkly interest-based terms of the labor movement or class-
based parties. Moreover, members of these movements are
mostly middle-class and educated – again, in contrast to the
working-class member base of the European labor movement
and its socialist parties. New movements tend to be about
themes related to life-style and identity politics. Today, the
politicization of identity and lifestyle is fundamental in many
social movements.

Interest in NSMs was slower to take off in North America,
partly because resource-based, organizational analysis still
had a lot of momentum, and partly because the labor movement in the US had taken a different course compared to that
in Europe. Socialist unions and political parties were not
major players in US politics, as they were in most European
states. Ralph Turner (1969) was one of the first US researchers to identify the rise of movements of identity and personal
transformation. Orrin Klapp (1969) also discussed a "collective search for identity" as a response to modern, rationalized social organization, which robbed people of stable
reference points for identity construction. The hippie movement of the 1960s exemplified the merger of identity quest

and lifestyle innovation among the younger generation, and had nothing to do with class divisions and inequality. Then in the 1970s punk collectives expressed a different lifestyle focus, but one that still embraced dress, behavioral codes, and living arrangements that were all taken as markers of a new antiestablishment identity. Like hippies, punk communes constituted a "submerged network" of countercultural lifestyles, which blurred the distinction between politics and daily life.

NSMs do not bear clear relationships to their participants' ascribed structural positions in society. Rather, their activism is grounded in new and diffuse social statuses – such as youth, gender, lifestyle, sexual orientation, or professions – that do not correspond with structural explanations (Klandermans and Oegema 1987). The network quality of these ties reflects the complexity of postmodern society and its organization, but also serves as the glue that binds new identities together. Today, members of urban communes and garden co-ops often share environmentally sustainable lifestyles, vegetarianism or veganism, bicycles, and natural-fiber clothing. Another way of thinking about these phenomena is that they are movements whose class or structural basis is less clear, and in the place of a compelling class-based and/or interest-based identity, they accord greater opportunities for self-definition to their members through new lifestyles and new, movement-based collective identities.

Della Porta and Diani (2006) define collective identity as a central aspect of all social movements, not just NSMs, because it plays a central role in coordinating protest behaviors. Gamson (1992b) observes that, if a movement is to endure, forging a strong collective identity must be a central task. Despite all the emphasis that the NSM approach places on collective identities, they are not strictly "new" to social movements. Striking Newcastle coal miners of the Nine Hours League in 1871, or Spanish anarchists in Madrid and Barcelona in the 1920s, strongly identified with their compatriots too. This identity was based on shared struggles associated with work and household, as well as activities in gathering places outside of work – pubs, union halls, and coffee shops. What is new is that NSMs mobilize on identities that are not associated with occupational status, class-based exploitation, and economic grievances (Melucci 1980, 1985, 1989; Kitschelt 1985; Kriesi 1989). These new identities are, in a sense, a product of postindustrial society in which low-level survival needs are more easily fulfilled and higher-level needs such as identity and self-actualization are given prominence.

Regarding the study of social movements, analysts looking at NSMs must consider the processes by which these movements generate their own unique beliefs, symbols, values, and meanings related to sentiments of belonging to a differentiated social group. This is "cultural work" based on interactional processes and microlevel performances, and, to study them, the researcher needs tools that are different from those appropriate for identifying opportunity structures, threats, and their effects. It is not surprising that scholars who kept alive social constructionist and interpretative approaches during the critical mass period – in the US, that would be the symbolic interactionist tradition – were among the first to contribute to NSM analysis. Studies of the women's movement, the animal rights movement, the environmental movement, and the punk movement exemplify this trend. I especially have in mind Verta Taylor's work as it applies to identity and performance in the women's and GLBT movements (Taylor and Whittier 1992; Taylor and Raeburn 1995), and Mary Bernstein's (1997) study of identity strategies.

Collective Identity

The concept of collective identity walks a tightrope between individual and social definitions. Psychological approaches focus on self-development and progress toward adulthood. Erikson (1968) notes that identity is a subjective sense of "continuity and being oneself" and he sees developing this sense as a fundamental step in growing up. More than in other stages in one's lifecycle, the search for identity is a concern of young adults. Erikson's fifth developmental stage occurs in late adolescence, when ascribed roles are reconciled with emergent adult roles. It is entirely plausible that there is a psychological, coming-of-age process at the foundation of many NSM groups.

In one of the seminal studies of the NSM perspective, Melucci and his colleagues (1984) analyzed groups that were composed largely of people between the ages of 18 and 28. In my own research among young political activists in Spain (Johnston 1991), I found that they struggled mightily to reconcile their traditional, often religious, middle-class upbringings with newfound commitments to radical social change. Identity reconciliation was a key theme among friends, especially through intense discussions of books that they all read, which challenged old ways of thinking. They also discussed revolutionary liberation movements in other parts of the world, and their personal struggles to develop a "working-class consciousness" when, in fact, they were all relatively privileged middle-class students. According to Hunt and Benford (1994), "collective identities are *talked* into existence." By this they mean that a movement's collective identity results from numerous interactions among participants, conversations about who they are, what they do together, and why. In these exchanges they offer up, test, and modify – according to the reactions of others – personal versions of what it means to be a group member. This is the process by which disparate meanings of movement membership and participation are brought under a broadly (and mostly) shared understanding.

In sociological approaches to identity, especially those grounded in the symbolic interactionist perspective, the relation of the individual to society is fundamental, to the extent that our self-awareness and even our consciousness are permeated by our social location. Concepts of the social self, the performance of social roles, and the ongoing confirmation of identity by others' reactions, based on the theories of George Herbert Mead and Erving Goffman, underscore the strongly social nature of who we are. The symbolic interactionist approach emphasizes that personal identity cannot be separated from its ongoing social construction and confirmation. This is a view that, as applied to social movements, focuses on the realization that collective identity, like self-identity: (1) is emergent – defined and confirmed in performances occurring at least partly in the context of movement activities; and (2) involves various audiences or publics, both internal and external to the movement. Identity-affirming performances can range from mundane activities – such as staff meetings, grabbing lunch together, or stuffing envelopes with other members – to the highly dramatic – such as protest marches, building occupations, strikes, and experiencing police repression and even imprisonment.

The concept of collective identity brings the performance dimension of culture to the foreground. Rupp and Taylor's analysis (2003) of transgendered performances shows clearly how acting out in drag is a way that collective identity is *performed* into existence. And for the audiences that are present, both among in-group members (the other drag queens) and out-group members (the cabaret audiences), the cumulative effect of these performances is to congeal the diversity of individual identities around a central hub of collective identity. It occurs through centripetal processes of in-group identity coalescence, and out-group processes of social definition and constraint, as imposed by others. Both internal and external dynamics shape group definitions into an identifiable core of collective identity – an ideation individually held – that is subsequently acted out and confirmed and/or adjusted according to the situation. In this sense, collective identity is a moving target.

Social movement research has confirmed ongoing social construction of collective identity on these two planes: internal to the movement among members, and external to the movement, among opponents, politicians, potential adherents, and bystander publics. Regarding the internal dynamics among movement members, Taylor and Whittier (1992) analyze the use of identity narratives among lesbian feminists to impart value to the collective identity and to politicize it. Young (2002) demonstrates that the nineteenth-century abolitionist movement used revival-meeting narratives among young Christians to build collective identities. Others have noted that participation in protests, risk taking, and shared fears work to foster collective identity over time (Pfaff 1996). Also, some researchers have argued that emotional responses to these actions strengthen collective identity, fortifying members for risk taking and for long-haul struggles (Goodwin, Jasper, and Polletta 2001).

We can see these processes in a statement of collective identity from a punk group in Minneapolis (see Johnston

PROFANE EXISTENCE

P.O. Box 8722 · MINNEAPOLIS, MN 55408 · U.S.A.
TEL. 612-377-5269 ·FAX 612-377-3866

WHO WE ARE AND WHAT WE DO: The Profane Existence Collective is a small group of revolutionary anarchists working together to produce a bi-monthly paper of revolution & resistance — not to mention punk rock. We do a record label, screen print shirts, run a literature and music distribution service and various other projects including local struggles and actions. All these things are anarchist in perspective and we do them with the goal of revolution.

WHAT WE BELIEVE: We ain't got no bosses and not one of us is higher on the ladder (what fucking ladder?) than any other. Some call this non-hierarchical we wouldn't have it any other way. We are anti-authoritarian, aim to kick the fucking cops out and keep them out, working for the total destruction of the state and capitalism and all the evil institutions they create. This system which we intend to string from the neck until dead divides us into classes based on power and wealth with the majority of people continually exploited by the rich bastards otherwise known as the ruling class. We support the rich in their numerous attempts at suicide, we might even throw in a helping hand. This fight is anti-racist and we support self-determination of people of color. We are pro-Queer, don't you know how sweet it is. We are anti-sexist with a swift kick to the groin of patriarchy. We support the fight for equality of those with different physical abilities. We fight against an ageist system in society that alienates the young and disregards older folks. We are eco-anarchists. We smile gleefully as multinationals burn to the ground. We will use all means necessary (i.e. the guillotine) to fight this oppression that fucks with our daily lives. Oh, and we'll do it with a smile. The revolution we fight for is one of pleasure to release us from the boredom of the everyday roles the ruling class has created. Have a blast while you drop the fucking bomb.

(DON'T) JOIN US: We don't think we are any higher than any one of you (remember that ladder? We burned it down). The last thing we want to do is lead any movement. We're not a party, we're having one. Do it Yourself, you and your friends, sisters and brothers can work together to solve the problems, take action, create autonomous zones. This is not some kind of dippy lifestylist drop-out commune thing but a situation for the spark of revolutionary movement with the aim of transforming our entire society. A society of freedom and pleasure, based on the needs and desires of people not tyrants. You got the power it takes to destroy the power that takes.

FIGHT BACK! A WHOLE WORLD IS WAITING FOR US!

Figure 4.1 Anarchist-punk manifesto of "Who we are"

2013 for a fuller analysis; also Snow, Johnston, McCallum 1994). Figure 4.1 presents a printed manifesto by members of Profane Existence, a punk-anarchist commune and a good example of a life-style-based NSM group. The manifesto proceeds with a litany of identity statements at the outset: "We ain't got no bosses"; "We are anti-authoritarian"; "We are pro-Queer [and] . . . anti-sexist"; "We . . . fight for equality"; "We fight against a . . . system . . . that alienates." These are strong antiestablishment sentiments that locate the collective within the anarchist-punk movement. But note that document is not a call for mobilization, nor does it make a statement about specific claims, nor is it an ideological tract, but rather it functions mostly as an artifact of the group's collective identity. At the end of the text, in the "What we believe" section, revolutionary struggle is conceived as a release from boredom: "Have a blast while you drop the fucking bomb." "We" are a "society of freedom and pleasure," less so for collective action on a set of claims and more so for commitment to a particular identity. While punks do protest – say, when local authorities move to restrict the group activities, close informal clubs, or empty building occupations – it is fair to say that lifestyle immersion into the local anarchist-punk scene captures the essence of punk identity (Leach and Haunss 2009). While other NSMs will differ in style and substance, the manifesto is a good example of how NSMs merge lifestyle choices and collective identity.

By their dress and demeanor, anarchist punks also put a lot of work into the maintenance of identity boundaries – who can pass as a member and who cannot. Kuumba and Ajanaku (1998) noted how dreadlocks at one time functioned as a marker of African nationalist identity, but as dreads became popular among those outside African-nationalist politics – not so much as a countertactic but as a fashion statement – their usefulness as a tag for identity decreased, and other means of boundary maintenance became necessary. Here, elements of collective identity change, not so much through an opponent's active resistance, but through benign changes in the social environment. In contrast, Robnett's (1997) study of the SNCC (Student Nonviolent Coordinating Committee) wing of the civil rights movement chronicled how the bitterly fought rejection of their platform by the Democratic Party at its national convention was a significant event in radicalizing members' collective identity. Here the boundary was partly imposed by movement opponents. Boundary maintenance occurs both ways – internally and externally. Because it is human nature to seek positive identities, the external efforts by opponents to stigmatize a movement group give rise to internal processes of valorization and affirmation.

Conclusion

It is tempting to speak of collective identity as something that a group has, but it is ultimately based on how members of a movement behave and talk among themselves – namely, what they do which defines how they think about themselves. Although a social scientist might compose a questionnaire to measure collective identity among adherents, it arises from the density and the frequency of relations that can be conceptualized as multiple microperformances of identity in the sense that doing things together reaffirms what we are together. If a movement is defined as a network of relations, a strong collective identity means that members are highly interconnected and their "identity performances" are frequent. Such performances are based on shared vocabularies, songs, and music, common experiences that are talked about and reminisced, ways of dressing and hair styles that present a self-image as a group member (Taylor and Whittier 1992; Meyer and Whittier 1994; Whittier 1995). In line with the approach to culture developed in this chapter, collective identity is an ideational dimension of movement culture whereby belongingness is defined in part by identity artifacts or markers, and affirmed continually and densely by small performances of who members are. The key insight of the NSM perspective is that when interests are less starkly apparent – as in groups with a greater emphasis on lifestyle and identity, and less emphasis on basic survival needs – collective identity plays a relatively greater role in the movement culture.

I close this chapter by returning to the observation with which it opened – namely, that while cultural processes and artifacts are deemphasized in some approaches to social movements, they are never absent. The compelling question for the field, then, is how much do these cultural elements play determining roles in the movement development and mobilization? Do their roles vary among different movements? As we saw in this chapter, some movements – especially those falling under the rubric of NSM – lay greater emphasis on the processes of collective identity, and the artifacts of membership and ideology. As we saw in the previous chapter, the contentious politics focus looks at movements that pursue group interests and that mostly navigate structural factors such as links with political elites, coalitions, and resources.

Yet all movements pursue social change goals (or oppose them), which imparts a fundamental contentiousness to all movement goals – both to NSMs and to more interest-based movements. You cannot challenge the status quo and awake the powerful forces that support it without being contentious. For the analyst studying social movements, a decision is always made – sometimes implicitly – about whether to focus on those structural elements fundamental to struggles over power, influence, and strategic action, or to focus on those cultural elements that are fundamental to group cohesion, perception of opportunities, and the symbolism of protest performances. Neither focus is inherently right or wrong. Rather, in the huge complexity of a social movement, an initial point of entry must be practically chosen. Moreover, with this decision comes a parallel choice about the methodological tools appropriate for cultural analysis (more on this in chapter 6), which often further exacerbates the division. Yet, this division is artificial in the full sense of the term – man-made, or woman-made – a matter of perspective rather than truth. The main point of this chapter has been that there are some movements for which cultural processes take a primary role, and that the concepts that are relevant for studying them are also relevant in varying degrees for studying movements that are more contentious and interest-based. The balance of these factors for explaining a movement's development is an empirical question to be hammered out on the anvil of research, and, for this to occur, dialog between the two approaches must be lively and sustained.

5
What Do Social Movements Do?

In this chapter I focus exclusively on the actions of social movements. This goes to the heart of what social movements are because marches, demonstrations, protest rallies, petitions, and sometimes violence distinguish movements from other forms of claim making. Political parties organize campaigns to mobilize voters and win elections. Corporations hire public relations specialists to shape public attitudes and lobbyists to influence policymakers. Social movements are distinguished by their unique repertoire of actions that work mostly outside institutional channels – the *modern social movement repertoire*. This concept embraces the full horizon of actions and tactics available to social movements today. In Tarrow's words (1994: 70), a repertoire is what protesters "know how to do and what others expect them to do." To understand what social movements do, then, a good place to start is with the basic repertoire of contention.

Charles Tilly (1995, 2006, 2008) played the greatest role in directing analytical attention to the concept of repertoire. He first discussed it (1978: 151–2) when the prevailing theoretical orientation was resource mobilization, a focus on interest-driven mobilization and its organizational basis. Tilly would later recall how an important theorist, Mancur Olson, once characterized the notion of repertoire as a "dangerous idea" (Tilly 2008: xiv), no doubt because its underlying cultural basis was at odds with widely held theories of the period. Tilly's (1995) historical analysis of contentious events in Great Britain from the mid eighteenth to the mid nineteenth century presented strong evidence for a basic shift in how protests were performed, a shift from a premodern to a modern repertoire. Later, as cultural perspectives gained traction in the social movements field, so too did the concept of repertoires.

Most actions in contentious repertoires are unconventional, dramatic, and lie outside the ebb and flow of everyday life. They are collective actions that require coordination, organization, and mobilization. They also are sometimes very dramatic and confrontational, and can grow very large, posing threats both to the police and to bystanders. The *logic of numbers* underlies many social movement actions. It is especially important because large crowds not only attract attention but also give an imperfect measure of public opinion to politicians and policymakers (DeNardo 1985). I say imperfect because a forceful minority can make demands that are not widely shared, but if demonstrations pass a threshold of drama and size, political elites take notice – the logic of the squeaky wheel that gets the oil. In democracies, elected officials realize that being responsive to public sentiments is necessary to remain in power. In nondemocracies, huge protests like the ones that occurred in Egypt in early 2011 disrupt daily business, divide elites, and sometimes topple the regime.

Media Performances

One way of thinking about the most visible actions in the social movement repertoire is to consider them as performances directed at certain audiences. A key audience in the twenty-first century is the press and broadcast media – and now social media and the blogosphere – all indirect brokers in influencing politicians and the public. To get mass media coverage, social movement performances also have to be compelling and dramatic. Researchers have recognized how important media attention is to movement success (Ryan 1991; Gamson 2004a, 2004b; Gamson and Wolsfeld 1993),

yet airtime and front-page space are limited. Social movements must compete with government officials whose
"inherent news value" is great (Gans 1979; Wolsfeld 1997),
which limits media access to political newcomers and challengers. Movement leaders must stage dramatic protest
events that are sufficiently media-genic to get 30 seconds on
the evening news. For example, the antiglobalization protests in Seattle offered photographers many compelling
images: giant puppets, street theatre, banners, and demonstrators in costumes. But the bar is always rising for what
media outlets consider dramatic and compelling. Gitlin first
observed this during the turbulent 1960s in the US. He
noted that simple marches and sit-ins made the news in
1965, but "it took teargas and bloodied heads to make the
headlines in 1968" (1980: 182). Also, the location of a
protest is a significant factor in whether the media pick it
up. Oliver and Myers (1999) observed that protests that
occur in major cities are more likely to be covered compared
to actions staged in out-of-the-way locations. "Making news
by making noise" has become a widely recognized tactic in
the social movement repertoire (Thrall 2006: 417). Moreover, as Gamson (2004a: 243) points out, the media not
only select what gets reported but also shape public opinion
by how they portray the protests and analyze them, which
makes media relations a significant element in the modern
social movement repertoire.

Performances

Tilly (2008) identified small-scale, bounded performances,
which he labeled *contentious events*; the sequential progression of these into larger clusters, which he designated as
protest campaigns; and then, the highest-level category, the
modern social movement, the broadest way of conceptualizing how contentious performances are aggregated. Social
movements embrace different campaigns, protest events, and
all the organizational, tactical, and strategic decisions that
go into them. These are decisions about what the protest
events look like (its tactics) and how they help achieve the

movement's strategic goals – in the short term, *campaign goals*, and in the long term, *movement goals* (Tilly 2008).

Protest performances are symbolic statements that work on numerous levels and in numerous ways. Not only are there the general issues about which the movement is making claims – their primary communicative acts – but there are assertions about who the various actors are, their relations with others, and their emotions. These are secondary communicative acts that are almost always present in protest performances, but which typically are more subtly asserted. Like other forms of communication, different channels are used to get these points across. Most obvious is the verbal channel that includes the chants, slogans, speeches, songs, petitions, leaflets, flyers, and press releases. But also there are the statements about identity, attitude, and emotions that are expressed through theatre, dress, posturing, dancing, art, masks, puppets, and other tactics. It is axiomatic that social movement performances are saying something to their audiences, but it is important to recognize how complex the messages are.

Tilly (2008; see also Tilly and Wood 2009) suggests a useful list to organize the basic symbolism in movement performances. Different movements will vary in the stress that they give these dimensions and not all will be present all the time. Also, within any given protest performance, different groups and organizations will emphasize them differently. Drawing on Tilly's observations, protest performances often includes displays of:

- *Worthiness* of the cause and of its proponents. Such displays are about the status of the members and are symbolically conveyed through dress, demeanor, deportment, and the participation of respected citizens, and perhaps even celebrities. Displays of worthiness also are indirect calls for public support by validating the participants' claims and asserting their right to make them. The mere collective act of gathering together so many worthy people symbolizes that the movement is a force to be reckoned with.
- *Unity of participants and of purpose.* Tilly points out that displays of unity are common in social movements. I would add that such displays are also a dimension of collective

identity. Especially in NSMs, such as those for gay rights or environmentalism, asserting group identity is a common display in protest actions. Unity (or solidarity) and identity are close cousins conceptually. They traditionally are displayed through disciplined and/or coordinated behaviors in marches and demonstrations. Costumes and similar dress, which historically were common among trade unions and different villages and locales, function as displays of unity and identity. Today, unity is communicated by signs and banners identifying groups in a march or a demonstration, by dress, by songs and chants, and by dramatic public behaviors.

- *Numbers.* Showing broad support is one of the most fundamental displays that a movement can make. The logic of numbers is directed at policymakers and politicians as a proxy of public opinion. Thus, some of the most recognizable elements in the social movement repertoire communicate the broad scope of support to audiences: marches and demonstrations that fill public squares and city blocks, and petitions with thousands of names. During the Arab Spring of 2011, the hundreds of thousands of protesters that filled Tahrir Square in Cairo communicated a powerful message of change to Egyptian elites in the Mubarak regime. The threat of disruption lies at the heart of how displays of large numbers assert pressure on established political structures. Recalling our earlier discussion, big numbers get media attention too.

- *Commitment.* This is a display that aggregates individual subjective states that reflect dedication to the cause. When members show commitment they convey to audiences that the movement is not a temporary phenomenon and that it is a force to be reckoned with. Because movements make claims and demands that impinge on the interests of others, it is important that participant commitment be clearly asserted in order to be taken seriously. Braving risks of police repression is a common commitment display. This is especially true in authoritarian regimes, where dissidents risk imprisonment, torture, and even death to oppose the regimes. Here displays of commitment also function as examples to others of sacrifice for the cause and break the conspiracy of silence that stifles opposition.

Emotional displays – often unplanned and reactive – also function as markers of commitment. Some leaders are distinguished by their ability to stir emotions among members to raise commitment. Researchers have pointed out the ubiquity of emotions in protest performances (Goodwin, Jasper, and Polletta 2001). Political alienation, anger, indignation, joy, resentment, outrage, even hatred are emotional states that protests commonly convey. Anger displays often take the form of property damage and violence, which raises the topic of the strategic use of emotions and, especially, disruption and violence as strategic decisions.

Regarding the general project of building knowledge about social movements, a focus on performances gives insight not into the whys of movement appearance and development, but into the hows of what they do. How do participants interact to give shape and direction to a course of action? How do protests develop? What role do leaders play? What is the role of the audiences who are present – bystanders and police? How do elaborations of the basic repertoire occur? Answers to these questions often take the form of both strategic decisions about the overall direction of the movement and practical decisions about tactics – namely, what to do and when to do it.

The Strategic and the Tactical

Dimensions of social movement performances are often decided upon at two levels – the strategic and the tactical. Social movement organizers strategize about the big picture of the struggle, considering long-term goals, such as passing legislation or invoking a regulatory response, for example closing down a nuclear reactor or monitoring the dumping of toxic waste. This kind of thinking is dependent on the degree of coordination among the various components of the movement and their willingness to reach common *strategies* on how to achieve movement goals. As part of a global plan, strategy decisions consider the political context of opportunities, allies, and threats, and commit to actions that take optimum advantage of them. That these decisions are deliberated and consciously taken, often in collaboration with participating groups, is a function of the modern social movement that is organized, complex, and goal-directed. One of the most fundamental strategic decisions a movement faces is the mix between noninstitutional strategies of protest and disruption and institutional strategies of political influence. The US women's movement strategized its efforts during the 1960s among an array of equality issues through a mix of protest and lobbying but when ratification of the Equal Rights Amendment to the US Constitution looked threatened, women's organizations concentrated on media strategies and lobbying state legislators whose votes were necessary for ratification. The strategic decision was taken that mass protests might alienate those few critical votes. Ultimately, the Amendment did not pass when the ratification deadline lapsed, failing to win approval by the required number of states. Its failure started much second-guessing about whether the strategic decisions were the correct ones.

Strategic disruption

The decision to pursue disruption, militancy, intransigence, and hard-edged tactics generally – including property destruction and violence – is fundamental to social movement strategizing. It is not surprising that researchers focused on this strategic dilemma early on in the field's development and continue to do so to this day (Johnston and Seferiades 2012; Bosi, Demetriou, and Malthaner 2014). Over 30 years ago, Piven and Cloward (1977) analyzed four cases of poor peoples' mobilization in the US, finding that disruptive strategies were more likely to help a movement attain its goals than nondisruptive, peaceful strategies. Their analysis emphasized the importance of vanguard groups that push hard and long against policymakers and authorities. Another influential study of the period was Gamson's (1990 [1975]) analysis of numerous challenging groups in the US. He found that, among other factors such as influential allies and resources, the use of disruptive tactics was instrumental in achieving movement goals. Taking these two studies a step further, one might infer that, if disruption is effective, then violent tactics – property damage and attacks on persons – may be more so. Given the rising bar of media newsworthiness, violence may be a strategic decision to get the media's attention.

The other side of the coin regarding strategic violence is that it runs the risk of alienating public opinion. Members of bystander publics and uncommitted groups comprise a movement's pool of potential allies, and a movement must be "carefully disruptive" so as not to scare away future adherents. Moreover, because movements are complex networks of groups, organizations, and individuals, there may be a few groups under the movement's umbrella that advocate radical actions while the majority may be strategically moderate. Protest and campaign organizers must balance needs of various groups that make up a movement with long-term goals – first, of maintaining membership, and second, achieving policy change. One study in the US shows a steady decline in property damage and violence in protests after 1967, when 33 percent of protests were violent and 21 percent caused property damage (Soule and Earl 2005: 353). By 1986, less than 10 percent of protests were violent and 2 percent caused property damage.

Strategic thinkers, especially in large movements, may take advantage of the "radical-flank effect." By leaving more militant groups to pursue their radical tactics – the anarchist Black Bloc, for example – the overall result for the movement may be "greater responsiveness to the claims of moderates" (Haines 1988: 171). From the perspective of policymakers, moderates are, after all, people that you can talk to, not "wild-eyed radicals." Just this kind of consideration occurred in the 1999 anti-WTO protests in Seattle, in which anarchists' unsanctioned end-run around more numerous tactically moderate groups that formed the campaign coalition helped attract media attention and public awareness to the campaign's overall themes (Smith 2002). Although violence did not by itself budge the WTO ministers or IMF officials, by punctuating protesters' commitment displays it may have forced policymakers to be more responsive to protesters' demands, especially loan forgiveness in the poorest countries.

Social movement tactics

"Tactics" refers to the concrete, short-term protest actions that are subsumed by a strategic plan. The term comes from the Greek root that means the "science of arrangement," which captures how activists consider which protest activities will best communicate the movement's demands and elicit a positive response from decision makers. Lunch-counter sit-ins (the civil rights movement), the AIDS quilt (the campaign to fund AIDS research), and the occupation of Alcatraz Island (the American Indian Movement) are all examples of tactical actions that make symbolic statements. Tactics that work get noticed by activists and are used again and again. When movement memberships overlap, tactics are shared. When the police develop their own countertactics, or the media do not judge a particular action to be newsworthy, unsuccessful tactics will not be repeated. Otherwise, it may be that small refinements of the tactical playbook are all that are necessary. These are numerous microadjustments that are easy for the analyst to miss or disregard as minutiae, but which neverthe-less are one way in which tactical repertoires are renewed and updated.

Figure 5.1 depicts a small example of tactical technology called a sleeping dragon. It was used by environmental activ-ists and has spread to other protests employing civil disobedi-ence, such as illegally occupying contested spaces. Protesters next to one another put their hands inside plastic PVC pipes and attach a carabiner clip (linked to chains around their wrists) to the crossbar inside the pipe. The purpose is to bind people together in a way that is difficult and dangerous for authorities to break. The logic is that authorities will not risk injuring activists by attempting to saw off the devices. By using it, activists display both commitment (facing risks and danger) and unity (being bound to others). Environmental activists linked by several sleeping dragons can form a human chain around an old-growth tree, for example, to impede its felling, or to stop the use of heavy construction machinery. It is an ingenious tactical apparatus that evolved through microlevel trial-and-error adjustments, such as using tar and chicken wire to impede the use of saws and obscure the

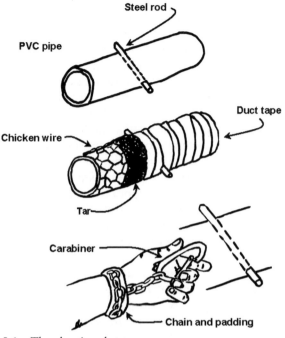

Figure 5.1   The sleeping dragon

device's weak point, the steel rod that protrudes on the sides. This back-and-forth between protesters, authorities, and – in some cases – countermovements represents the principle of very small-scale tactical dynamism.

How Repertoires Change

In contrast to these microscopic changes, the general bundle of performances that constitute the *modern social movement repertoire* – marches, speeches, meetings, demonstrations, petitions, strikes, occupations, and more – have evolved through macrolevel shifts in the state and governance. Their appearance parallels the emergence of the modern, high-capacity, national state, of national markets for production and investment, and of the complex division of labor characteristic of industrial society. Traditional society was predominantly rural, and landowners and magnates were the local governing authorities. Governance at the national level was fragmented and limited in its territorial reach. The way people protested then would be scarcely recognizable today. The *premodern repertoire* was predominantly local in focus, limited in duration, and often quite dramatic in how it took direct action about grievances and claims.

Traditional protest actions typically focused on injustices of the landowners, unfair or burdensome taxation, and rising food prices. It was common that villagers expressed their discontent with high prices or unfair taxation by direct action – property damage, setting fires, or seizing goods. In England, a common action was the destruction of fences that enclosed fields once open to villagers or forests that were a source of game. Grain seizures from the storehouses of merchants who were suspected of hoarding or unfair pricing were common. In these cases, community outrage was immediate and focused. A merchant might be subjected to public shaming such as "donkeying," "rough music," or "charivari." Donkeying was a public punishment in which villagers paraded the offender – often hooded or seated backwards – through the village while the crowd hurled insults and garbage. In rough music and charivaris, villagers gathered at the offender's house to sing songs and shout taunts. Although these collective actions appear to be spontaneous and disorganized, they in fact helped set the boundaries of community morality and were strongly modular – even ritualistic.

Tilly's (1995) analysis of changing protest repertoires in Great Britain in 1758–1834 led him to summarize the premodern repertoire in three ways. It was *parochial*, meaning that it was based and focused on local grievances and injustices rather than national ones. It was *particular*, namely arising from immediate pressing issues such as food shortages or outrage at an arrest or press-gang conscription of the village men. Finally, it was *bifurcated*, an uncommon term which needs a little explanation. Because the premodern state relied on local nobles, landowners, or magistrates for governance of areas distant from the capital, these authorities enjoyed a great deal of autonomy. Premodern protests were aimed mostly at them, and they often could take appropriate action on their own account. In some cases, however, villagers' demands and petitions were to the King or Parliament, and needed to be relayed by local authorities because there was no direct line of appeal or representation. Thus, a two-step (bifurcated) line of claim making, first local then national, took appeals to the King or Parliament.

As democratic state regimes became institutionalized, a certain configuration of tactics emerged as the best way to pursue collective claims. This process is captured by Tilly's notion of a *strong repertoire*: "like the style of a theatrical performance, participants in contention are enacting available scripts . . . as a result, repertoires acquire causal and symbolic coherence" (Tilly 2008: 59–60). Yet strong repertoires are not set in stone. As much as political and structural contexts channel protest tactics to standard forms, tactical changes are also driven by creative and autonomous participants with the capacity to innovate. In some cases they innovate for its own sake – a reflection of their innate creativity. In other cases they do it because the evolving, real-time protest situation requires it. Perhaps the police have been called out in force and occupy an adjacent street, or counter-protesters congeal unexpectedly, which requires a tactical adjustment. Tilly used the metaphor of a jazz performance where, within the broad contours of known melody, the various players creatively improvise, influenced by each other and by the audience's reaction.

The Diffusion of Social Movement Performances

Tactical repertoires change through innovation and creative adaptation, but researchers have also noted that they often change through borrowing. The adoption of an innovation or new idea via interpersonal relations is a process called *diffusion*. It has been studied in the social sciences since the 1940s, especially regarding the purchase of new products or the adoption of new technologies, but only relatively recently have researchers recognized the role of diffusion in social movements. The concept applies not only to tactics (McAdam and Rucht 1993; Soule 1997), but also to the spread of ideologies, beliefs, traditions, and frames (Snow and Benford 1999), and to what would appear to be the wildfire-like spread of protest events to other geographical areas (Myers 1997), which can give rise to large-scale cycles of protest (Tarrow 1998).

The growing incidence of ties among social movements and movement organizations that function on the global level – environmentalism, global justice, peace, and human rights movements – has alerted researchers to the transnational dimension of diffusion, although it is not new. The signature tactic of the civil rights movement, nonviolent direct action, can be traced to how Gandhi used nonviolence against the overwhelming force of the British in the Indian independence movement (Chabot 2000). Early African-American leaders had traveled to India to meet Gandhi and his compatriots. Others who studied the Indian movement and read its literature were closely linked to King, Abernathy, Shuttles, and other preachers, for whom nonviolence meshed nicely with their Christianity. Early in the movement, this overlap was important in convincing participants of the utility of nonviolent tactics. These principles of interpersonal contact, ideological compatibility, and the exchange of ideas through print and broadcast media are key elements of tactical diffusion present in many contemporary movements.

Direct diffusion

One way that diffusion works is through direct personal contact among activists. Shared, overarching goals within a movement give occasion for leaders and activists from different groups and SMOs to communicate. These are opportunities for tactical innovations to be passed among member groups and organizations. Also, it is not uncommon that, given the network basis of movements, some activists are more central than others, meaning that they have several, overlapping memberships in different groups. Intramovement diffusion may occur through seeding of tactics from one SMO to another through central figures and opinion leaders. These individuals often play the critical role of *innovators* or *initiators* of new ideas or behaviors among their personal networks. Other times, the initiators of innovations may occupy somewhat peripheral locations in the networks. In these cases, their contacts with centrally located *early adopters* are the first steps in an innovation's journey to gain acceptance.

It is common that activists from different organizations come together to coordinate specific campaigns, rallies, or protest events. In these situations, another diffusion role comes to the foreground – namely, that of *brokers* who can transfer information among people who were previously unconnected. Through brokers, networks are extended and members have opportunities to talk shop about ideas, strategies, and what tactics work, and under what circumstances. Brokers can play a crucial role because it is common that competition for resources, membership, media attention, and ideological and strategic influence exists among various movement groups, which means that there may be a tension in these networks. But activists and leaders frequently think about how to get their messages across effectively, and brokerage can be a key mechanism whereby diffusion occurs (McAdam, Tarrow, and Tilly 2001: 332). Snow and Benford (1999) observe that the brokerage function can be intentional on the part of centrally located individuals, and an important dimension of transnational diffusion. The potential of the brokerage mechanism expands exponentially in the internet age, when, through blogs and social media, brokers can play instrumental roles in diffusing new ideas without face-to-face contact (Givan, Roberts, and Soule 2010).

Intermovement diffusion can occur in much the same way. Meyer and Whittier (1994) coined the term *social movement spillover* to capture how activism in one movement sometimes overlaps with that in another, with the effect that tactics migrate among different movements through these multiple roles. Their analysis points to a common phenomenon in progressive social movement circles – namely, overlaps in membership. For example, Meyer and Whittier note that members of the women's movement who also were active in peace protests in the 1980s were a source of tactical similarities between the two movements. Other researchers have found that spillover effects between the feminist movement's campaigns to combat violence and LGBT movement's antiviolence initiatives can partly be attributed to key players active in both movements (Jenness and Broad 1997). Soule (1997) traced the diffusion of a unique tactic from one movement to another: student occupations of university spaces by erecting "shantytowns." She also found this tactic was transmitted through membership overlaps in the student movement and, later, in antiapartheid protests that focused on divestment of university endowments in South African companies. Direct diffusion is sometimes reinforced when there are strong parallels regarding political philosophy and/or ideology among movements. Shantytowns sprang up in many of the large global justice protests in the 1990s. When movements have divergent ideologies or political philosophies, a different kind of diffusion operates: *indirect diffusion*.

Indirect diffusion

In the contemporary era when the mass media provide far-reaching and immediate coverage of protest events, it is common that activists get ideas for new tactics through print and broadcast sources. This is the case when movements share tactics but their mobilization periods do not overlap (which reduces the likelihood of simultaneous memberships). Although there was scant overlap in membership, the nonviolent tactics of the civil rights protests of the 1950s and 1960s – sit-ins, boycotts, and provoking mass arrests – were picked up by the Chicano movement and by antiwar student groups in the 1970s. That these groups shared broad social change goals with the civil rights protests encouraged the borrowing of tactics that they saw on television years earlier. In the 1980s, these tactics were also adopted by movements at the other end of the political spectrum, most notably the antiabortion movement and a powerful organization that was part of it, called Operation Rescue. Indirect diffusion through the media is especially important during periods when there is an upsurge in protest activities. Tarrow (1998) has observed strong patterns of overlap in tactical repertoires during *cycles of protest*, even among opposing groups. His discussion suggests that, during these times, indirect, media-based diffusion is a fundamental mechanism in the *modularity* of protests within these cycles.

In practice, modularity is reinforced by a combination of direct and indirect diffusion, as occurred during the 1960s cycle of protest when student mobilizations spread across the United States, Western Europe, and Latin America. This was a period when student anti-Vietnam activism in the United States generalized into a broad antiestablishment ideology of resistance against state authority called the New Left. In Europe, the roots were different, but here too a momentum gathered on university campuses and culminated in huge student protests in 1968, especially in France during May of that year. There was a strong modularity among many of the student mobilizations: meetings, marches, building occupations, free-speech spaces, and property destruction, reinforced through common identification with other students' struggles and a broadly shared New-Left ideology. This was a time when air travel was costly – but not infrequent – which worked to limit direct contact among student leaders and participants, but it was also the heyday of the new medium of television. As the title of Gitlin's book (1980) on the media and the New Left suggests, "the whole world was watching" when students occupied Columbia University and when French students almost brought down the government during *le mai français*. While McAdam and Rucht (1993) chronicle limited instances of direct contact among leaders in antinuclear protests, it is fair to say that the media were the key mechanism behind the diffusion of tactics in student protests. Students at the National Autonomous University of Mexico in Mexico City acknowledged that their protests in September 1968 were partly shaped by student mobilizations in Europe and the US (Harding 1969), even though the demands uniquely reflected Mexico's history and politics.

This discussion of modularity carries with it two warnings. First, modularity does not preclude creativity. The Mexican students also innovated tactics, most notably a respectful and nonviolent silent march of 30,000 through city-center streets to gain public-opinion support – a very prudent tactical decision by student leaders. Second, although we are focusing on the diffusion of tactics, there are other movement elements that also diffuse. Ideological similarities also occurred among the various student movements of the period within the broad contours of a Leftist-oriented, antiestablishment critique. Technically, the process is labeled as a convergence under a broad, ideological *master frame*. Also, among student movements, an organizational form based on consensus decision making diffused as well. The point here is that not only do tactics diffuse, but other elements that define social movements do too.

If we seek to explain why some tactics diffuse more easily and rapidly than others, ideological similarities and the gathering of movements under a shared master frame provide many answers. They facilitate contexts for intermovement coalitions and crosspollenization (Meyer and Whittier 1994). Also, broadly shared social change goals facilitate recognition of useful tactics among activists from different movements. Although I have discussed that progressive and conservative movements sometimes share tactics based on the utilitarian principle of "if it works, use it," in practice, movement groups will weigh utilitarian criteria against ideological considerations, sometimes rejecting tactics "tainted" by their origins in opposing movements. Polletta (2002) notes this process in the organizational coalition of the Seattle anti-WTO protests, which rejected certain tactics they deemed as "masculinist," and adopted organizational tactics of deliberative democracy and consensus decision making that were consonant with their beliefs. Della Porta (2009) points out that the adoption of the key provision of the deliberative democracy organizational model for the World Social Forums is guided by ideological considerations of consensus, equality, and the public good, characteristic of progressive organizations.

Repertoires and Regimes

Although Mexico today is a democracy, in 1968 it was a one-party authoritarian state with a tendency to repress protests, which translated into a tragic ending for the student movement mentioned earlier. On October 2, 1968, thousands of peaceful students were surrounded by 2,000 army troops at the Plaza de las Tres Culturas in Mexico City, and dozens of tanks closed off streets leading in and out. Troops opened fire on trapped students, killing or wounding hundreds. Thousands of students were arrested that night, crushing the student movement for some time. This kind of military force applied against unarmed students is reminiscent of the Tiananmen Square massacre in China in 1989, when – by some estimates – 5,000 peaceful protesters calling for democratic reforms were killed. China too was a repressive, authoritarian state that limited protest activity, and remains so to this day. Although not all states would so readily call the army out against peaceful students, it is important to recognize that some do, and that, more broadly, there is a range of tolerance among different states and regimes that strongly affects strategic and tactical decisions of social movement activists. This gives rise to a different repertoire of contentious actions in repressive states, an observation that has significant consequences when social movement researchers direct their attention outside the democracies of Western Europe and North America.

Recall that the emergence of the modern repertoire was linked with a shift from traditional autocracies of kings, lords, and landowners to modern democratic polities. Tilly (2006) identifies two dimensions of state structure relevant to repertoire type: state capacity and degree of democracy. The shift from premodern to modern repertoire occurred as a result of increases in both dimensions. States with low capacity have limited control over territories. Sometimes, administrative authority is dispersed among local power brokers, landowners, and militia leaders, whose allegiances to the center are weak and unreliable. In some states, there are areas within borders where administrative authority does not extend at all – hinterlands, badlands, and "wild wests" where bandits roam and roads are unsafe. Tilly's point is that, where state capacity is weak, movements tend to challenge the state directly, as in armed insurgencies and separatist rebellions. Western democratic states are high-capacity regimes in the sense that state authority penetrates broadly and deeply into all citizens' experiences.

The dimension of democracy is more familiar and apparent. Like state capacity, democracy can be treated as a variable and analyzed by four basic measures. First, different states will exhibit different degrees of citizenship rights that are granted to inhabitants. Second, they will also differ in the degree of access to political representatives, and, third, in their responsiveness to citizens' demands. Fourth, they will vary in the legal protections offered to citizens. Regarding social movements, the application of these four parameters translates to a state's prevailing strategy toward tolerating protest actions (Koopmans and Kriesi 1995). Outside of Western democracies, tolerance is often very low, and reflected in the size and density of the social control apparatus. It is common that authoritarian regimes, especially those that are higher on the dimension of state capacity, commit significant state resources to the police and military to control dissent. In Syria, for example, the al-Assad regime had no less than 18 separate police and security organizations operating in major cities. This made for a very dense, *high-capacity*, social control apparatus. In contrast, democratic states in most cases honor citizens' rights to voice political dissent. As long as protests take place within legal parameters, police and security forces restrain the use of force, and may even facilitate protests that have permits. Modern democratic states are high-capacity too, as evidenced by the fact that police presence is taken for granted at most protests.

The repressive repertoire

Protest repertoires in authoritarian states, where political dissent and public protesting can be dangerous to life and limb, are very different from those in states with democratic openness. High-capacity authoritarian states seek to control political discourse by penetrating citizens' daily activities to insure compliance with official policies and to squelch dissent before it grows. Under these circumstances, the main damper on protest mobilization is fear. Kuran (1995) suggests that political discourse in authoritarian states is governed by *preference falsification* among its citizens. He observes that fear of fines, harassment, police beatings, and imprisonment prevents people from speaking their minds, which creates a conspiracy of silence based on conformity among people afraid to speak against official policies. While preference falsification is widespread in repressive regimes, it is never complete. Research shows that there are always a handful of people who are willing to risk a great deal to speak the truth. Most apparent among these activists are well-known dissidents – scientists, poets, lawyers, and artists – who bravely voice public criticisms of the regime. Playing on their notoriety, they dare the regime to take action against them (Johnston and Mueller 2001) and risk international condemnation. But there are also many others who, although they may be unknown and risk less, play a crucial role in the overall configuration of the opposition by how they help break the conformity of silence. How this occurs is central to the *repressive repertoire*.

The importance of these ordinary citizens lies in that they perform two key tasks: (1) they create *free spaces* that are outside the surveillance of the regime – these spaces become locales where activists gather privately and speak the truth (as opposed to the official "double talk" which makes up most official discourse and public speech); (2) they plan small collective actions to move the opposition beyond the restrictive and often secretive organization of these free spaces into public spaces – and try to do this without getting caught. To avoid capture, they introduce a third element into the repressive repertoire: (3) in early stages of the movement there is a great deal of innovation, creativity, and risk in tactics.

The authoritarian state cannot conceivably penetrate all aspects of daily life to monitor everything that everybody says. True, people must be very careful in public speech, but this can be managed by limiting political talk to trusted friends. Using this tactic, free spaces can even be carved out in groups and organizations that are officially recognized but which secretly can serve as forums for oppositional talk. In my research in several authoritarian regimes (Johnston 2006, 2011), people I spoke to had no trouble identifying groups and organizations known for their veiled oppositional milieu. In the minority republics of the USSR, folk-dancing groups, choral societies, ethnographic study groups, folk music groups, theatre groups, local historical societies, and drama clubs typically performed this role. Elsewhere, excursion groups, outing groups, geography associations, and even bee-keeping clubs (!) were sites of political discussion. These *duplicitous groups* are relatively few and the actual threat they pose to the state is minuscule. Their main effect, however, is quite significant: the careful oppositional speech that occurs in them allows members to know that they are not alone in their discontent. This tears the veil of silence common among citizens in repressive states, and keeps oppositional sentiments alive so that when political opportunities open (say, through division among elites or international pressures), there is a pool of potential participants who are available for more public performances of protest. While audiences are limited for these performances, they set the stage for the next level of participation.

If repression levels weaken and/or activists become bolder, the second set of tactics unfolds within the repressive repertoire. There is a pattern of innovative actions that have the same effect as duplicitous groups – namely, keeping alive oppositional discourse – but expand their audiences further by breaking into the public realm. *Clandestine placements* are actions that are risky, often highly creative, and expand the audience of challenging performances. Examples are secretively painting graffiti and political slogans, or placing flowers, flags, banners, crosses, candles, or other oppositional symbols in highly visible locations. An example – with symbolism that is hard to miss – occurred when students in the former USSR placed excrement in the outstretched hand of Lenin's statue and a loaf of bread in the hand behind his back. In Syria, opposition activists poured red dye into fountains in Damascus to symbolize the blood spilled by the al-Assad regime. Activists also placed in trash bins stereo players that repeatedly played revolutionary songs. A different kind of placement recently occurred when a newspaper artist in China drew a cartoon to commemorate Children's Day that had hidden references to Tiananmen Square, any public discussion of which is strictly prohibited. The cartoon, which ran three days before the Tiananmen anniversary, showed a child's blackboard drawing of tanks and a figure standing in front of them – an allusion to the iconic images of the sole student who blocked tanks at the protests – and the torch of democracy. The editors who approved the cartoon placement lost their jobs.

Figure 5.2   "Commemorating Children's Day" at Tiananmen Square

Another tactic in the repressive repertoire is an *event seizure*. These are innovative acts of protest often planned by small groups of activists that again push the symbolism of challenge and resistance into the public eye. They take advantage of collective gatherings to turn them into relatively safe occasions to voice oppositional sentiments. For example, the "spontaneous" singing of prohibited political songs at public concerts or sporting events is one kind of event seizure. The diversion of funerals is another. It is common that funerals of well-known dissidents or martyrs for the cause are given strong political symbolism well beyond the mourning of a death. The politicization of funerals in Gaza and the West Bank, and the diversion of their routes, frequently occurred during the Intifada uprising. A different kind of event seizure occurred in the 2009 prodemocracy green movement in Iran. Although the movement was heavily repressed, during warm summer nights in Tehran people often gather on roofs of city buildings. This social practice was "seized" in 2009 when one could hear the movement's slogans shouted from roof-tops across the city at night. There was little the police could do as calls echoed through the city streets.

Each of these tactics bears witness to the broader public that there is an opposition out there. For those who despair at the unresponsiveness, corruption, and injustices of the authoritarian state, such knowledge must be heartening. Many of these tactics offer relatively safe tastes of protest participation to previously uninvolved publics. In this way, they help redefine in small ways new political possibilities for the wider population. Moreover, it is common that the small, high-risk groups that organize these actions are schools for future movement leaders (Johnston 2006). For all these reasons, the more the state is unable to quash these forms of protest, the more it runs the risk of broader protest mobiliza-tion down the road. In time, these actions begin to take on the more recognizable tactics of the modular social movement repertoire characteristic of democratic states.

I close this chapter by noting that the primary audience for these performances is less the elites of the regime and ruling party than the repressive state's unengaged bystander public. This distinguishes the repressive repertoire from the modern repertoire in democratic states, where the primary targets are policymakers and politicians, and where the public and media are secondary targets through which to exert pressure on the primary ones. But there are no perfect democracies, and when elected officials vary in their responsiveness – by policy issues, by region, by system of governance, and by prevailing policy of social control – the audience mix changes and the shape and content of social movement performances will vary. These final observations about the repressive repertoire serve us well to highlight how a performance-oriented per-spective brings the challenger–audience dynamic into the analysis, which can offer important insights even in demo-cratic states.

Movement performances almost always occur in the theatre of state systems. They not only are shaped by the opportunities and threats posed by the state, but also shape them. The nineteenth-century extension of political represen-tation did not occur because of political elites' commitment to democratic governance. Rather, emerging movements pushed for wider political representation, as Tilly showed regarding Catholic representation in 1823, and as the woman suffrage movement later pushed political elites to change. This dynamism also occurs as movement leaders plan tactical shifts to make the movement's image resonate better with the public or increase its newsworthiness. As in theatrical productions, social movement performances also have to be compelling and dramatic to capture the attention of their audiences, and, depending on the state where the performances occur, the audiences will differ. But the bottom line is that there are always intended audiences for social movement performances, primary and secondary, and they make a difference. This observation goes to the heart of the performance metaphor. For the collective actions of social movements, Shakespeare's line from *As You Like It*, "All the world's a stage and all the men and women merely players," always holds true. In the words of one activist pondering the fate of his movement, "Like you'll find in anything, you can't stick to the same thing. . . . You cannot be static, and you have to change your tactics" (Schmidt 2012: 19). He was speaking about the fate of the Occupy Wall Street movement. "We need to keep them guessing," he continued, referring to a fundamental strategic imperative of social movement performances: to keep the audiences' attention.

6

Researching Social Movements

There are numerous approaches to the systematic study of social movements, each of which, if done well, has the potential to advance our knowledge. Careful research methodology is what sets social science apart from personal or impressionistic accounts of social movements. The difference is that social scientists are professionally committed to getting it right. By using established methods of data collection and analysis, a study's findings and how they were arrived at can be closely examined for biases that may have skewed the results. Typically, published research reports describe the authors' methods. If other scholars disagree with the findings, how the study was done is often a target of close scrutiny.

Looking at the broad horizon of the social movement field, one needs to be attentive to methodology. By choosing a theoretical question – say, why participants join, why movements are successful, or how protesters interact with police – the analyst is pointed to certain methodologies and away from others. The other side of the coin is true too: sometimes researchers are committed to certain methodologies, and the tools one prefers tend to direct one's theoretical focus toward some aspects of a movement and away from others. These two observations mean that the relation between theory (directing what gets studied) and method (choosing ways to do it) is fundamental to what one sees in a social movement. The relationship between theory and research methodology is also dynamic, not only in these terms in planning a project and choosing a methodology, but also because each affects the other during the data collection and, sometimes, right up to the final analysis and write-up.

There are three fundamental groupings of ways to study social movements: historical-comparative methods, qualitative methods, and quantitative methods. I will look at each from an altitude of 30,000 feet, meaning that I will describe the general lay of the land as we fly over, identifying the important landmarks. In this book, this means relating them to the three main dimensions of studying social movements from the first chapter: ideational, structural–organizational, and performative. Some methods are especially poised to give insights into one dimension or another, while in other cases, different methods give different perspectives on them, or can avoid them entirely. Methodological choices have potentially profound consequences for the topography of our field of study.

Historical-comparative Research

Historical research is not necessarily comparative, but it often is, which explains why the two terms often occur in tandem. One way of looking at the comparative dimension is that a focus on long-term views of history – say, over a century or more – frequently forces the analyst to confront variations over time. Differences in separate time segments then can be compared to identify key variations, which then are often correlated with shifts in state structures or economic organization – which also requires long-term historical data. Historical-comparative methods are especially well positioned to give insights into the structural elements in social movement development in the context of changing state structures.

Contemporary history – say, a focus of 25 to 50 years prior – is, of course, no less "historical" than ancient history, but the shorter timespan does mean that data sources are different. Some of the most significant contributions to the field are grounded in contemporary history: McAdam's (1988) analysis of high-risk activism among Freedom Riders used archives where applications from university and college students to participate were stored; Morris's (1984) study of the origins of the civil rights movement used both archival and oral histories as sources. The list of major studies in the social movements field grounded in contemporary history, using a variety of data sources, is very long.

Comparative-historical approaches also include research that analyzes crossnational data as a systematic way of testing hypotheses about the causal relationships among two or more political variables. Looking at the distinct political structures in one country and comparing them with another's can recast a county's political institutions as independent variables, for example when multiparty parliamentary systems are contrasted with two-party presidential systems to see whether protest levels are affected. Generally speaking, making such comparisons with the goal of explaining differences in political outcomes – the dependent variables – is the general logic of comparative politics, a major research subfield in political science. It is not surprising that many political scientists interested in social movement issues choose crossnational approaches to contemporary cases.

In this vein, there is a long tradition of historical-comparative political research that seeks to understand the structural prerequisites of revolutionary movements, insurgencies, and political violence. Such research may consider large historical time frames with an eye to grand, macrostructural shifts, such as the development of prerevolutionary conditions in eighteenth-century France or nineteenth-century Russia. Research on revolutions also may take a crossnational approach, such as comparing the Mexican and Chinese Revolutions. Historical-comparative research sometimes constructs systematic databases from archival sources or official data to statistically analyze long-term trends. For example, measures of state repression can be standardized across several national contexts by gathering data on deaths, arrests, police budget expenditures, relative size of security forces, and so on. These are then correlated with protest levels. In the 1960s and 1970s, historical-comparative researchers working in this quantitative vein extracted measures of deprivation and frustration crossnationally for correlations with political violence. Although these are social-psychological factors, the focus was on the structural causes that lay behind them, with the presumption that they drove protests. However, as della Porta observes (2002: 290), statistical analysis of this sort is often difficult to apply to studies of national-state structures because of inconsistencies in data sources and imprecision in official data.

William Gamson's seminal study of protest strategies (1990 [1975]) followed this logic. He began by producing a comprehensive data set of 453 "challenging groups" in the US between 1800 and 1945. He then sampled a group of 53 for intensive analysis, which was done by using a questionnaire to gather theoretically relevant information from a variety of archival, newspaper, and scholarly sources. The research strategy was to statistically analyze the effects of organizational variables, measures of institutional strategies, and engagement with the media, police, and so forth, on the success or failure of newly mobilizing groups – the dependent variable.

A similar methodological strategy was applied to large and complex archival data by Charles Tilly, to study, first, strikes and collective violence in France (1986) and then collective action repertoires in England (1995). In both projects, Tilly constructed data sets – in the French case, spanning 1830 to 1968, and in the British, from 1758 to 1834. The research designs aimed to chronicle cases of contention that met certain criteria for the given time periods: a huge task. In France between 1830 and 1968, there were about 110,000 strikes that were counted and coded. Here, official records were especially helpful, and French newspapers and political yearbooks were used to augment the list. Also, the study enumerated about 2,000 violent events with property or personal damage in which at least 50 persons participated, either challengers or officials. Tilly's studies combined historical-archival research, comparisons between time periods and countries, and event analysis that, where appropriate, applied statistical modeling for comparisons.

Like Gamson's study of organizations, it was a huge task to systematically list and describe contentious events, and this was only part of it – the studies' dependent variables. Tilly's main research goal was to trace how macroscopic structural shifts in political, social, and economic organization affected the shape of collective action in France and Britain. To present a case for causal relationships, measures of changes in social structure (urbanization), and shifts in the organization of production (capitalism), and in politics (elite conflicts, suffrage), were needed for the period.

For the student interested in exploring further the research decisions and protocols, Tilly offers 50 pages of appendices that trace them in detail in his book *From Mobilization to Revolution* (Tilly 1978: 245–306). Gamson's *The Strategy of Social Protest* (1990 [1975]) also has a large and comprehensive methodological appendix. In a broad sense, these cases of historical research (and many others, e.g. Voss 1993; Gould 1995; Clemens 1997) show that "social movements themselves are historical accomplishments of particular kinds of societies" (Clemens and Hughes 2002: 223; also Buechler 2000: 3–11).

Qualitative Methods

Some observers judge qualitative methods to be less scientific, more journalistic, and/or more preliminary approaches to social movement research. Such a perception rests on the fallacy that the relatively greater standardization of data-collection strategies and of analytical tools based on probability statistics imparts the greater objectivity. As we saw in the last section, quantification sometimes involves great creativity in bridging data gaps. And in the next section, we will encounter how survey research must deal with bored interviewers, reluctant respondents, differing interpretations of questions, mistakes, and outright misrepresentations. In fact, all data are, in a sense, qualitative at the point where they are produced in the sense that subjective judgments and interpretation almost always enter in. Qualitative methods are simply different tools that researchers use to get at different questions. They give especially useful insights about the lived experiences of movement participants, the reasons for their participation, the decisions they make, how they see their actions, and the impacts their actions will have. The analyst can explore these elements with other methods too, but not with the depth of qualitative methods.

Participant observation

As the label participant observation (PO) indicates, the researcher becomes a fellow traveler with the subjects he or she is studying. The researcher takes part in protests, meetings, social gatherings, informal chats, and everyday activities – and constantly reflects upon what it all means to participants. But, also, the PO researchers must reflect upon recurrent patterns and take their analysis to a higher theoretical level. This is the process of making social science out of lived experience that lies at the heart of PO. In a recent study of anti- and pro-Iraq-war protests in the US, two researchers (Oselin and Corrigall-Brown 2010) attended opposing protests every weekend in California for a period of several months to ascertain the forces that shaped how the protests unfolded. They got to know the protesters, participated with them, talked to them about reactions from passers-by, all in order to stand in their shoes, to see the protest context from their perspective, to understand why they behaved as they did. The result was not a journalistic insiders' report of pro- and anti-war protesters, but a detailed chronicle of what was said, events, backgrounds of participants, and interactions that were translated into the concepts of social movement theory: a delineation of various determinants of tactical choices in protests that are generalizable to other instances. The authors had to continually alternate between their role as participant and their role as researcher – specifically, taking notes, reviewing them, looking for patterns, and thinking about theoretical linkages.

The overarching goal of PO is to be able to see the world from the perspective of the other participants. The rationale is that, without understanding their point of view, it is impossible to know what motivates their actions. PO is a method closely identified with the theoretical perspective of symbolic interactionism, which emphasizes the collective definition of situations as central to understanding human behavior. PO gives insight into the *how questions* of social movements by sifting through the diversity and complexity of collective interpretations of a group or at a site to identify generalizable processes. While PO cannot answer all questions that interest social movement researchers, it is especially geared to answering questions of motivation, collective definitions, and the ideational dimension of social movements. PO gives the field of social movement and protest research insights that surveys, event analysis, and historical-comparative analysis typically cannot.

Amy Austin Holmes (2012) was a participant observer in the tumultuous 18 days of Egypt's January 25 Revolution that overthrew the country's authoritarian leader, Hosni Mubarak. As a professor at the American University in Cairo, she did what any dedicated social movement researcher would do in those early days of 2011: she immediately went out to the streets. She attended the mass protests. She hid in apartments, observed the sweep of events, the ebb and flow of conflict. She was assaulted by police in one instance, and was protected by fellow protesters. She spoke to participants, and, throughout, repaired to private spaces when she could to make notes on what she saw and heard. Imagine the temptation to be swept up in these historic events, cheer the cause of freedom, vilify the police and thugs of the regime, and lose the perspective of the analyst. Austin Holmes's research is a poignant example of a dilemma that all PO researchers face: losing analytical distance through identifying with your subjects and their definitions of the situation.

Note too that, unlike the planning of coding protocols and construction of databases in historical-comparative research, or the testing of questionnaires and identification of sampling frames in survey analysis, this example of PO had a less systematic and a more spontaneous and developing quality to it. This emphasis on the developing and emerging identification of patterns and theoretical understandings is another characteristic of the PO method. But this also raises the problem that, without guidelines to direct the participant observer about what to look for, the danger is that his or her unique perspective will bias the findings. Continual self-reflection, bracketing of one's expectations, and working with others are ways to identify one's presuppositions and keep them from coloring one's analytical eye. Lichterman (2002) recommends writing them down as one of the first acts in taking field notes. By noting one's presuppositions and theoretical expectations, the researcher can use them as benchmarks for reflection upon the theoretical progress of the study and how they influence what has been observed and recorded. This constant self-reflection on theory, on analysis, and on whether one is biasing the analysis is a characteristic of PO that is very personal.

For the participant observer, one's field notes are the "hard data" which serve as the basis for identifying higher-level theoretical processes after leaving the field. For the researcher, a lot of one's heart goes into those notes – they are about relationships, shared thoughts, and common experiences over extended periods of time. Sometimes, some very private observations go into them, and researchers must be protective of their subjects (see Blee and Taylor 2002). Personal involvement in ongoing observations can also compound questions of objectivity. However, PO's ultimate justification – like that of event analysis – is that it gives insights into social processes that no other method can and thus justifies the risk.

Intensive interviewing

Intensive interviewing is often called *semistructured interviewing* because it is flexible and open-ended in gathering responses. It moves according to a general outline of themes and probes for important information, but also allows for going with the flow of the discussion to explore areas that open up during the session – perhaps topics that were not anticipated by the researcher. For this reason intensive interviewing is sometimes used as a preliminary step in planning a research project, especially survey questionnaires. However, the insights from in-depth discussions with the subjects often are significant by themselves. Research based on intensive interviews alone is not uncommon in the social movements field, and, indeed, some very influential studies were done this way.

Survey researchers, of course, interview hundreds, or perhaps thousands, of subjects. Intensive interviewing projects, in contrast, typically do not go above 100. I have seen published reports that base their findings on as few as 20 respondents, but, as a general rule, that is probably too few for anything more than raising provocative theoretical questions. In my research in the former Soviet Union, working with another colleague, we did about 100 in-depth interviews with oppositional activists, and in my research about nationalist movements in Spain I conducted 80 interviews. The rationale is that more respondents offer opportunities to double-check reports and confirm patterns of interpretation and accounts. Most of my interviews lasted about an hour plus, but they can go on for longer. Taylor states that some of her interviews lasted up to four hours, no doubt a reflection of her interviewing skills in developing trust and drawing out respondents (Blee and Taylor 2002).

Central to these size-of-N questions is that intensive interviewing must strike a practical balance between number of respondents and several time-consuming steps: (1) lining up and doing the interviews themselves; (2) the transcription of the interviews (a common but highly labor-intensive task); (3) the close analysis and interpretation of responses that, unlike in surveys, are often not sequential or systematic; and (4) consideration of the additional quality of natural speech that sometimes buries pearls of insight deep within narratives about other topics. This last factor imparts an extra, time-consuming constraint: some interviews may be very difficult to analyze, requiring acute linguistic and narrative sensitivities to make sense of various levels of meaning and performance embodied in them (Johnston 1995, 2002).

The richness, depth, and insightfulness of information gathered from intensive interviews are strong counterweights to concerns about sample size. Intensive-interview data offer perspectives into social movement processes regarding the cultural construction of meaning and interpretation, and how participants accomplish these – information that surveys and event analysis can rarely access. Insights into questions of identity, crisis, and life's big decisions can be illuminated through intensive-interviewing methods if the interviewer can establish trust and rapport with the subjects.

These qualities are unique to the method, and all are relevant to three genres of intensive interviewing, which sometimes overlap in research projects. *Oral histories* elicit recollections of events, movements, or protests past. Blee and Taylor (2002: 102) observe that oral-history interviewing is especially useful in documenting events that have been understudied or missed by official histories, often the activities of marginalized groups, "difficult" groups (see Polletta 2006b), or groups to whom access had not been available (such as Blee's 1991 study of the women in the Ku Klux Klan). *Life-history interviews* are personal narratives, often audio-recorded, that focus on the life events of individual participants in social movements (della Porta 1992). They reflect theoretical interest in the individual's lived experience in the movement, their activities in events and organizations, their reactions, emotions, and interpretations, and less so in the events and trends themselves. Finally, *key-informant interviews* are with people who know a great deal about an important event or organization or played central roles in a movement's history. In my own research, the relationship between these last two genres can be seen. While collecting oral histories, I was unexpectedly led to several groups as sites of "hidden resistance" to the Soviets: folklore groups, choral societies, and outdoor hiking clubs. A subsequent step in my research was to identify key informants who were involved in these groups and who might be willing to discuss their activities. By treating them as key informants, I was able to identify and chronicle several unrecognized aspects of the political opposition in authoritarian regimes. The interviews provided evidence for a deeply hidden aspect of politics in repressive societies (Johnston 2006).

Quantitative Methods

Quantitative methods make two presumptions that, although not uncontested, are taken for granted by most social scientists: first, that social forces are big and work on a large scale, and, second, that they can be measured by aggregating individual cases into numerical trends. This macroscopic vision of social relationships and change means that analysts must collect large numbers of data points so that overall patterns and tendencies can be discerned. In the study of social movements, these are typically numerous responses about participants' decisions and/or ideas, or numerous protest events and their attributes. To get from the myriad inputs of raw data to manageable numbers, the analysis involves steps of data reduction, categorization, cleansing, and summation, before tabulation and/or statistical analysis can be applied. In the social movements field, two main styles of quantitative methods are survey analysis and event analysis.

Survey analysis

Survey research gathers information about social actors – voters, activists, and even organizations when questions are posed about their activities. The information gathered by surveys is then grouped or aggregated to give a picture of the collectivity and its composition according to theoretically relevant categories. Survey research is a key tool in contemporary social science, and has been called the signature method of sociology. There are several excellent book-length guides to survey research (Babbie 1990; Alreck and Settle 2004; Lavrakas 2008; Fowler 2009). This section will focus on the particular issues related to surveys as applied to social movement issues.

For most surveys, the individual is the unit of analysis, which, for us, means social movement participants. The main data-gathering tool is the questionnaire distributed to large numbers of respondents, either personally, by mail, by email, or on websites. Questionnaires are sometimes used as guides by which telephone interviewers ask questions of the respondents. End-of-term teaching evaluations for professors are written survey questionnaires, although students probably fill them out online. Each student's answers are aggregated with other students' responses and the results tabulated by the questions. It is typical that questionnaires pose specific fixed-choice questions such as "How would you rate the organization of the class?" or "How many protests have you participated in?" In surveys about protest participation, typical questions ask about motivations, attitudes, identification with the movement participants, goals, ideology, friendship ties, participation in other groups, and knowledge about the movement's goals. It is not uncommon for questions to ask about future intentions to protest – although intentions do not always align with actual participation. Such information is often analyzed according to subgroupings based on age, sex, education level, income level, profession, and so on.

Unlike student teaching evaluations, which are completed by all students in the class, a common element in survey research is that the respondents who are questioned usually represent only a proportion of the total population. This is a major benefit of surveys as a social research tool. They offer a way of saying something about large populations by gathering information from smaller groups. One can do this if – and it is a big "if" – one can be secure that the subpopulation selected is representative of the total universe. Two related issues in selecting a sample are that it: (1) be large enough to give sufficient data inputs in the subgroupings that interest the analyst; and (2) be selected in a way that the researcher has confidence about the sample's representativeness.

The first point is pretty straightforward, limited only by the resources available to the researcher, which are always practical constraints operative in making research decisions. Regarding the second issue, researchers commonly rely on methods of random selection, which then enable statistical techniques to predict the level of confidence about generalizing to the overall population. Bringing these two issues together, most political surveys and election polls have only 1,200–1,400 respondents to represent a universe of millions of voters, but they are *very carefully chosen* – not necessarily randomly, but often based on models of demographics of the population in question. While there is a science in constructing a representative sample nonrandomly, there are risks. In the 2012 US presidential elections, Republican challenger Mitt Romney's polling was inaccurate, misleading him to anticipate victory. In contrast President Obama's extremely large sample of 29,000 in Ohio, based on models of likely voters, gave accurate predictions of victory there.

Researchers often rely on nonrandom sampling when access to membership lists is not possible, or when the protest phenomenon is less organized, or when research is exploratory. In these circumstances, snowball sampling can be used, in which initial contacts provide names for subsequent contacts, who then do the same, and so on. If played through to the end it can produce quite large samples, but they have a network quality that can systematically exclude segments of the population and overemphasize others. The main drawback of nonrandom sampling is that probability statistics cannot be reliably used to assess the representativeness of the findings and analyze them. Random samples require a comprehensive list of population universe, known as the sampling frame, from which a sample is drawn. In the absence of such a list, which is not uncommon, the researcher must begin with what is available and then take extra steps to construct a more complete sampling from various other sources.

Given the importance of SMOs in contemporary social movements, organizational surveys designed to map contemporary movements are not an uncommon research design. The difference between organizational surveys and regular surveys is that organizations, not individuals, are the units of analysis (Klandermans and Smith 2002). In contemporary organizational surveys, a common procedure is to send officers of NGOs and SMOs questionnaires, or to question them by telephone. Typically, theoretical concerns guide questions about organizational goals, number of members, relations with other SMOs, protest participation and mobilization, resource use, organizational structure, and so on (Dalton 1994; Minkoff 1995).

Survey research can be applied to numerous types of research questions important to the social movements field. Besides cross-sectional analysis of participation and of SMOs, survey data are highly relevant to network analysis of movements to trace the interconnections among organizations (Diani 1995; Diani and McAdam 2003; Von Bulow 2011) and/or among their members. A network perspective guides analysis but is not itself a data-gathering technique. Network analysis is equipped to answer many important questions in the field of social movement research: recruitment, patterns of participation, diffusion, movement trajectories, and strategizing, all based on network locations of organizations and how these influence decisions movements make, or, more generally, the network configurations of the movement as a whole. Survey research is a key methodology to gather this kind of information (for methodological elements of the network perspective, see Diani 2002).

A final observation is that some survey analyses do not collect their own data but rather use the work of other researchers and/or research organizations that have greater resources and can conduct large national studies. Research analyses that rely on precollected data must adapt to the fact that they do not design their own questionnaires or choose their samples. The question of how well the available data synchronize with the study's theoretical concerns is always relevant, but with creativity in thinking about relationships and correlations, and by knowing which data might be mobilized as evidence for correlates, the use of precollected surveys is not an uncommon strategy in the social movements field. Among the best-known precollected sources are the national censuses and surveys of the major North American and Western European countries, which can be useful in crossnational comparisons of political and economic contexts. Also, there are periodic surveys of public opinion, economic expectations, religious attitudes and attendance, and political behavior and attitudes that can be used in conjunction with data on movement activities to assess the influence of political and social context on mobilization. Yet such studies always need measures of social movement activity if the analysis is to argue causal relationships, which brings us to our next topic: event analysis and the construction of large databases based on newspaper reports. These studies collect reports of protest over periods of time sufficiently long to permit assessment of trends in protest activity and to test what factors may be correlated with changes.

Protest-event analysis

Protest events are the "command performances" of social movements. They are the primary means of getting the attention of political elites and policymakers, and of swaying public opinion. Contemporary protest-event analysis looks at the broad landscape of such performances, often in a given country, or comparatively in several countries. Depending on how the research question cuts, it can say something about a specific movement and its mobilization processes, but it is a method better suited to studying the dynamics of how protest performances develop and change (Tarrow 1989).

Such research questions require information about large numbers of protests over long periods of time. The main method to gather this kind of data is to take reports of protests, demonstrations, marches, collective violence, and so on, from newspapers, although other sources such as police records and official governmental reports are sometimes used. Today, a common practice is to apply sophisticated statistical analysis to test models of how different variables are related to each other, or how event-specific variables (e.g., size, frequency, themes) are related to macrosociological variables such as regime type, political opportunities, or protest cycles.

In recent years, the trend has been that large and well-funded projects examine more and more newspaper reports for more and more information – that is, coding for more and more variables – which means closer and deeper scrutiny of each individual article. Gathering hundreds of thousands of data points on tens of thousands of protest reports requires a large, well-trained, and stable research team. It has been observed that protest-event analysis has grown into a small research industry (Koopmans and Rucht 2002: 233) – perhaps an exaggeration, but certainly it has employed hundreds of research assistants and dozens of leading investigators in recent years. One of the first "protest-data factories" was located at the Social Science Center in Berlin, the PRODAT (for "protest data") Project, which sought data on all forms of protest in Germany since 1950. A plausible estimation of the total universe of events would have been over 50,000. To limit the task, the project sampled reported protests in two established and respected newspapers by reviewing their Monday issues every fourth week. This yielded about 14,000 protest events and a large number of variables, such as size, place, duration, issues, claims, primary and secondary targets for the protests, and related events (see Koopmans and Rucht 2002 for a general summary; also Rucht, Koopmans, and Neidhardt 1999).

There were several other large projects similar to PRODAT: a crossnational study of NSMs (Kriesi et al. 1995) which also used the strategy of Monday-only sampling (more on this shortly) to gather information on about 7,000 protest events in France, Germany, The Netherlands, and Switzerland. Then, there was a study focusing on ethnic claims and immigration in Europe, which sampled newspaper sources in five European states (see Koopmans and Statham 1999). Then, beginning in 1997, a project called Dynamics of Collective Protest in the US, led by Susan Olzak, John McCarthy, Doug McAdam, and Sarah Soule, aspired to assemble the largest protest-event database yet. Borrowing aspects of the PRODAT design to permit eventual comparisons, the US study aimed to examine all issues – not just Monday issues – of the *New York Times* from 1950 to 1995 in two phases, beginning with the turbulent years of 1960–80. To date, several research reports have been published based on the data that have been codified so far (Soule and Earl 2005; McAdam and Su 2002; Wang and Soule 2012). The huge size of the Dynamics of Collective Protest database permits large-scale trend analysis as well as single-movement analysis. The database is large enough for a single-movement subsample to still yield a sufficient number of cases to do a robust analysis. In addition to these major projects, there are many "mom-and-pop" shops of protest-event analysis that typically focus on one country's major newspapers, and sometimes just a particular movement or kind of protest. A selection of some of the best would include Almeida (2008, El Salvador); Shefner, Pasdirtz, and Blad (2006, Mexico); White (1999, Ireland); Kousis (1999, Greece); Beissinger (2002, the former USSR); Olzak, Beasley, and Olivier (2003, South Africa).

Despite the growth of protest-event analysis as a methodology and the numerical leverage that taking newspapers as a data source gives the researcher, it is an analytical strategy not without critics. The logic of protest-event analysis rests on how the data sources – in most cases newspapers – reflect the reality of protests for the period under study. Sampling is one source of error, but this can be corrected – if resources are available – by examining all the newspaper issues, as the Dynamics of Collective Protest project does. But there are

other sources of bias that go to the very heart of how newspapers report news. For example, the *New York Times* is
often used because it is a paper of national prominence, but
does "All the news that is fit to print" – as the *Times*'s motto
goes – include protests that occur in San Diego, California or
Milwaukee, Wisconsin? One possible answer is to use more
than one paper, but would including the *Washington Post*
and/or the *Los Angeles Times* solve the problem about San
Diego? There is an inherent bias in major newspapers regarding location of protests.

There are other biases present in national newspapers,
such as ideological filtering, standards of newsworthiness and
impact, available space on any given day, and the bottom line
of the newspaper business, selling newspapers. These are
called *selection biases*. Simply stated, the most comprehensive
list of protests from the most prestigious of national newspapers, "newspapers of record" as they are sometimes called,
is not the same as the total and true universe of events for a
given time period. Numerous selection biases have been identified in national newspapers. They generally fall into two
general categories: (1) those that derive from characteristics
of the event; and (2) those that reflect choices made by newspapers or wire services.

Regarding the first, there are several factors that increase
the likelihood of newspaper coverage (McCarthy, McPhail,
and Smith 1996; Mueller 1997; Barranco and Wisler 1999;
Oliver and Myers 1999). Primary among them is how close
the newspaper or wire service is to the protest event. Returning to our San Diego example, there is a very high likelihood
that the local *San Diego Union Tribune* would report the
renters' strike, but coverage would decrease in more distant
newspapers. Size of protest has been found to be a major
factor in press coverage. Local papers provide much greater
coverage of smaller protests, whereas for national papers,
participation of 10,000 marks the threshold for coverage.
Studies have shown that, below that number, coverage drops
to well below 50 percent.

Regarding editorial decisions, it is more likely that protests
will be covered if they use dramatic tactics, are sponsored by
large SMOs, use violence, have counterprotesters present,
and are related to topics of public interest – an impending

decision to go to war, for example. McCarthy et al. (1996) observe that factors related to the "media attention cycle" tend to reduce coverage. Editors think that public interest fades during sustained protests, and so will decrease their coverage as time passes. The overall conclusion is that newspaper data pass through a "newsroom filter." Newspapers systematically exclude smaller protests and events by resource-poor groups – in other words, protests by sectors that are socially marginalized, perhaps in poor urban neighborhoods, or by minority and/or ethnic groups with little political clout. Missing these would have significant effects on how we theorize about social movements.

By now, the student might be wondering, given these multiple biases, what is gained at all by protest-event research. To answer this, it is important to step back and remember that the study of social movements and protest is social science, not physics or chemistry. It is the nature of the beast that our measures will *always* carry *some* biases with them. Thus, the critical question becomes, if one is interested in trends over time such as size, themes, changes in repertoire and/or forms of mobilization, and looking at these trends crossnationally, how else are these topics to be studied? Event analysis is simply the best method available for these questions, and researchers are always looking at ways to improve the collection and analysis of protest data.

There are methodological innovations that offer solutions to some of the selection biases. First, if the biases occur systematically, statistical adjustments can correct for them (Hug and Wisler 1998). Second, text-recognition programs, first applied to comprehensive news sources such as Lexis-Nexis or Reuters, can facilitate building a comprehensive sampling frame of protest events. Advances in automatic analysis of grammar have been applied to protest-event analysis, for example the PANDA project – Protocol for Assessment of Non-Violent Direct Action. These programs, plus sheer number-crunching abilities of computers with rapid processing speeds, allow researchers to dredge through mountains of newspaper texts – local, regional, and national – to construct really massive databases that can mitigate selection biases based on spatial factors. The Kansas Event Data System (KEDS) began applying this logic to automatically analyze international conflict events over 20 years ago (Schrodt 2006), and it was applied to protest events soon thereafter (Bond et al. 1997). Students can visit http://eventdata.psu.edu/other.html for a list of the various protest-event datasets.

A final word is in order regarding this brave new world of digital analysis. Social media, such as Twitter and Facebook, and digital communication technologies based on smart phones open new avenues of research based on really huge communication flows. While these are not data typical of protest-event analysis, for the social movements field, track-ing communications during protest events holds great poten-tial for identifying relationships and patterns. We will discuss how digital technologies are used by activists to mobilize protests in the next chapter, but, for the researcher, the task is to sort through the billions of data bytes that flow among thousands of devices to identify basic trends. This can be accomplished relatively straightforwardly regarding who is talking to whom, which is important information, for example, when looking at network-oriented questions such as the diffusion of protest tactics and organizational patterns (Wang and Soule 2012). By the way, tracking talk patterns is what security agencies in the US were/are doing to identify terrorist networks. When documents were leaked in 2013 about government surveillance of mobile phone data in the US, a huge controversy ensued about encroachments on free-doms. Social scientists, of course, do not have the resources that the NSA applies to tracking calls to al-Queda operatives or safe houses in Pakistan, but the future portends the appli-cation of huge data-processing programs to all communica-tions flowing during a protest.

However, more complex questions typical of protest-event analysis ask not only who is talking to whom but also – by analyzing the talk – who is doing what to whom, where, and why. Regarding these questions, automatic processing of digital data is developing rapidly, but because the production and interpretation of meaning is a human act, controversies occur among proponents and detractors of large-scale digital "data scrapping" methodologies, even though most practitio-ners recognize their limits. The "weak link" (and the greatest drain on resources) in the large-scale event analysis of the past was human coding of raw event data. The ideal is to take the human element out of the equation through computer programs that can do the interpretation for you. To date, this has been accomplished partly by programs that identify the basic subject-verb-object relations of lead sentences and headlines in newspaper reports and on websites, but questions of reliability remain when compared with human interpretation of the same text. This is because texts are layered, often occurring within lengthy narratives, with themes, subthemes, and subtleties regarding tone and symbolism. Identification of how all this fits together to convey a text's metatheme almost always requires human interpretation. One approach to narrative complexity is quantitative narrative analysis (QNA), which has been applied to social movement research by Franzosi (2004, 2010) and De Fazio (2013), yet here too, human coders are needed to deconstruct the layers of narrative before the computer programs can go to work.

❧❧❧

For all the methodological approaches discussed here, most researchers would agree that the best we can do is to seek good evidence for our ideas, maximize objectivity, and minimize the biases (or at least clarify for others where biases may lie) so that the work-in-progress quality of our theory building can be nudged forward. Although some postmodernist scholars would reject this quest for scientific objectivity (see Johnston 2010), all would agree that a quest for accuracy in supporting arguments is fundamental. Reviews and exchanges among the community of social movement researchers are key elements in "getting it right." They help identify entry points of bias and error that otherwise might go unidentified. As a researcher, I have been asked to provide interview transcripts to other scholars to support my interpretations, and gladly do so. Openness about one's data is the standard, not the exception. This also is why high-quality, peer-reviewed journals such as *Mobilization* are the gold standard of reporting findings in the field. Prior to publication, submitted research reports are read closely, evaluated, and their findings weighed by anonymous experts who judge a study's worth and accuracy. This is called the double-blind peer-review process, and is the standard method used by the best academic journals to evaluate research. Although there is a professional dedication to reporting valid and accurate research findings, there is also a professional norm that recognizes a reliance on other social scientists to judge whether we have been successful or not. In the pursuit of truth – and even in the pursuit of the answer to the question "What is truth?" – we rely on other professionals to check our enthusiasms and biases, because, after all, we are human. Of course, they are too.

7
Where are Social Movements Headed?

In the twenty-first century, the pace of social change will be rapid. Primary among the drivers of change is the digital revolution in information and communication technologies. Starting with the internet and email in the mid-1980s, and then the proliferation of smart phones, tablets, social media, and Bluetooth in recent years, these technologies are changing the way we live and relate to each other. It is estimated that 2.5 quintillion bites of data are created daily, and that 90 percent of the data that exist in the world today have been created in the last two years. In the hands of social movement activists, new digital technologies can encourage and facilitate mobilization, helping to extend the scale of protest beyond past limits of geography and culture, and shrinking the time required for coordinating protest tactics to a flash – as in "flash mobs," those instant collective actions convened by texting and tweeting.

Digital technologies have potentially profound impacts on the relationship of states to social movements. Historically, popular movements have played key roles in prodding the responsiveness of political elites and resisting autocratic tendencies. Movements of the past have won the vote for excluded minorities – Catholics, immigrants, disenfranchised blacks in the American South, and women. Indeed, without popular protest, it is fair to ask whether the modern state would reflect the degree of democratic participation that it does today. In nondemocratic states, where political institutions are often ossified, corrupt, and fail to provide basic services and protections, social movements are the primary vehicles whereby popular calls for change can be expressed. State regimes and social movements have always been in a dynamic relationship. Based on mass mobilizations in recent years, there is good evidence that the digital revolution puts this relationship into high gear.

As change-oriented NGOs and advocacy organizations become larger and more professional, can these new technologies keep protest movements vibrant and contentious? Can they move them into new areas of freedom and empowerment, and to new levels of challenge – say, at the global level? In nondemocracies, can new technologies enable social movements to challenge corruption and the restrictions of freedom, or will the same technologies be used for their cooptation and repression? These are the questions that I will pursue in this final chapter as I plot social movement trends. The implications for the field of study are profound, as some scholars ponder whether new technologies are changing the social movement repertoire fundamentally.

Digital Mobilization

In the mid-1980s, activists began to see the internet's utility as an organizing tool. Like a fancy corporate letterhead or an address in a prestigious building, a website could confer legitimacy on the smallest and fringiest of movement groups and offer an inexpensive way to spread their messages to huge audiences. All that was needed was a web domain, which could be maintained at a relatively low price compared to the costs of printing leaflets, petitions, and posters – the main information media that SMOs used in the past. Websites were a significant advance regarding the *informational dimension* of mobilization, and they remain so to this day.

Soon organizers recognized the *networking dimension* of the internet as well. Websites and listservs could help build constituencies and collective identities among people with no personal contact but who shared grievances and/or claims.

The internet enabled organizers to transcend the limits of geography, the diffuse distribution of injured parties, and the absence of face-to-face interaction (Myers 1994). Victimized groups, marginalized citizens, and discriminated-against populations, such as victims of pedophile priests, AIDS sufferers and activists, ex-Scientology members, ex-Mormons, ex-Roman Catholics – and the list goes on – could build online communities and identities, give support, and – importantly for our purposes – organize actions. The same effects, often with legal consequences, were available to fringe, extremist, and awkward groups such as the Ku Klux Klan, right-wing militia groups, Islamic mujahidin, and the North American Man/Boy Love Association.

The decade of the 1990s might be called the classical age of internet activism. In addition to the informational and networking functions, possibilities for wholly *web-based activism* that was quick, easy, and inexpensive became apparent. For example, the Rainforest Action Network site had a feature that could send faxes in the name of the website's visitor to policymakers and executives of logging corporations calling for protection of old-growth forests. Similarly the National Abortion and Reproductive Rights Action League (NARAL) site facilitated the sending of emails to politicians in support of their cause (Kriemer 2001). In 1999 MoveOn.org began as an online campaign to urge the US Congress to "move on" to the business of governing during the Clinton impeachment hearings. Using chain emails, its online petition gathered more than 500,000 names. MoveOn. org quickly became an established player in progressive politics, hiring a paid staff and branching out from petitions and emails to use multimedia approaches, including print ads, and the latest web technology for presenting video clips, audio files, and graphic downloads. Yet at its outset, the organization was notable for how its website offered an easy way to get involved for thousands of "five-minute activists" (Raney 1999).

A different kind of web-based activism also appeared among techies, computer nerds, hackers, and open-source advocates. I have in mind various forms of hacktivism (or electronic civil disobedience, as some call it), for example flooding opponents' websites or diverting visits, sending "email bombs," publicly shaming opponents, or changing website banners, photos, and content. Some hacktivists go beyond pranks to steal information and release it publicly, or to infect opponents' websites with viruses or worms. On the one hand, many of these examples are new digital variants of old-time tactics of sabotage, graffiti, and whistle blowing. But on the other, a new kind of virtual actor seems to be emerging, one who is part of an antiestablishment subculture that militantly defends the internet's transcendent qualities as free, accessible, spontaneous, collaborative, leaderless, self-organizing, and (mostly) beyond the control of the state. I jump ahead several years to refer to the Anonymous network, which is wholly internet-based, wholly virtual, with no face-to-face contact, yet it is able to organize against threats to internet freedom (as in hacktivist campaigns against the Cybersecurity and Internet Freedom Act in 2011) and in support of open-access causes and progressive actions (such as attacking child porn websites, supporting the Arab Spring, and aiding the Occupy movement).

The questions these sorts of actions pose to social move-ment research begin with what kind of collective action do we have here? What dimensions of collective identity can be found among Anonymous participants? Can a virtual network be sustained without face-to-face contact and without long-term commitment? How are these virtual activities related to the personal connections, meetings, and in-the-street pro-test gatherings that have been the signature activities of col-lective actions in the past (Earl and Kimport 2011)? Such questions suggest a brave new world of collective-action forms that push the modular social movement repertoire in new directions.

Social media and the modular repertoire

The relation between virtual and traditional protest actions has come to the forefront in research about the Arab Spring, during which social media such as Facebook, YouTube, and Twitter were used in huge popular mobilizations. The Arab Spring of 2011 was made up of several people-power upris-ings against repressive regimes in the Middle East and North

Africa: Tunisia, Egypt, Libya, Yemen, Bahrain, and Syria. Most important for our purposes are the successful movements in Tunisia and Egypt, where mass protests eventually led to regime change after national military elites intervened in support of protesters' demands.

In both these countries, the progress of mobilization and the changing alignments of internal political forces were complex and had their own unique trajectories, but a common thread was the use of the internet, internet-based communication technologies, and especially social media in mobilizing popular opposition (Alexander 2011). Just a year before, widespread protests in Iran used similar means to mobilize against fraudulent elections, so the penetration of these technologies to the Middle East should not have come as a complete surprise to observers. Although uneven in their economic development, many of these countries have sizeable urban middle classes, and, especially among the younger generation, many people are technologically smart and web-connected nationally and, in some cases, globally. Howard (2010) notes that internet usage has been increasing rapidly in the region, but involves only about 17 percent of the population. Through those who are internet-linked, however, a two-step connectivity works to expand the role of social media, first through internet-based networks, and, second, through face-to-face social ties of those who are connected with their extended families, neighbors, and friends.

Analysis of digital media's role in Egypt and Tunisia is still underway, but preliminary results indicate that it is incorrect to say that these were wholly internet- or Twitter-based revolutions. Rather, social media played a supportive role, and the traditional face-to-face networks spanning family, friends, and neighborhoods were primary in mobilizing people in the streets. One study suggests that, much like internet-based, international solidarity networks for movements like the Zapatistas, Twitter was used to "actively and successfully engage an international audience in the Egyptian revolution" (Wilson and Dunn 2011: 1269). Also, usage was concentrated among a small group of "power users" – bloggers, journalists, and activists – who were connected with a large second-tier group who received their content and retweeted it to others in their networks, sometimes adding their own content and words of support. Regarding actually getting people into the streets, the same authors suggest that Twitter and shared knowledge of its global reach contributed to the motivation and morale of protesters, although the analysis is preliminary. Coordination of protests, passing of news of police movements, informing about the fast-changing elite-level developments, and updates from mass media such as Al-Jazeera and Alarabiya, all occurred through widespread mobile phone usage among protesters, as did retweets and texting to journalists and the uploading of street-level photos to international media. The digital dimension occurred alongside and as a complement to the real-time protests in Tahrir Square, and it was the sea of participants, the threat they posed, and the disruption they caused – and not their tweets – that forced the hand of the military to depose Mubarak.

The bottom line is that first the internet, and then the Web 2.0, are important additions to the tactical toolbox of the modular social movement repertoire. Their use will only increase, and they will continue to have significant effects on the informational and networking strategies of future social movements. Yet, much of what we have seen so far is a tactical extension of trends that researchers already have identified. For example, the checkbook membership of the Worldwide Fund for Wildlife or Greenpeace can now be accomplished online with PayPal, credit cards, and phone accounts. Movement marketing can be accomplished via website tactics (e.g. pop-ups and banners for Amnesty International). Professionalization of media strategies now includes forays into Facebook and Twitter, release of web videos, and getting coverage by online news sites. The vast networking functions of the internet open new possibilities of "five-minute activism," such as online petitions and email campaigns, but these are fundamentally expansions – greatly enhanced by technology – of established tactics of hand-signed petitions and letter writing. It remains a question for future research whether the staying power of movements that rely on virtual recruitment matches that of movements based on traditional face-to-face ties. Recall Tilly's simile (2008: 14) that the modern social movement repertoire is like jazz improvisation that occurs within the guiding melody of an old standard. These internet-based "lines" and "phrases," improvisations on a basic tune, are mostly tactical innovations that synchronize with and enrich the larger melody of collective action traditionally understood – the modular social movement repertoire.

Transnational Movements and the Internet

The 1990s were years of global protests, and it is not coincidental that, to bridge the geographical dimension inherent in global issues, activists expanded greatly the information and networking functions of the internet during the same period. However, it is important to recognize that the transnational dimension of social movements is not solely an artifact of the internet. Technological changes in the nineteenth century were first steps in the intense space–time compression that characterizes globalization processes today. For example, Hanagan's study (2002) of the transnational dimensions of the Irish nationalist movement argues that trans-Atlantic steamship routes played a crucial role in creating immigrant communities that could support the movement at home. During the same period, international organizations, such as the Universal Postal Union (1874) and the International Bureau of Weights and Measures (1875), which fostered standardization and international exchange also were established, precursors of the powerful multilateral, global organizations of 100 years later. Businesses that operated in different countries increased greatly into the twentieth century, setting the stage for social movements that recognized the international character of corporate exploitation, a trademark grievance of the global justice movement of the 1990s.

At the heart of the global justice movement was outrage at the unfairness of global manufacturing operations. Huge protests worldwide were organized against the policies of multinational organizations such as the IMF and World Bank, which encouraged international business under the banner of the neoliberal free trade regime. Prior to the digital revolution (that is, in the 1960s and 1970s), anti-imperialism, anticolonialism, Fidelismo, and international communist, socialist, and revolutionary movements certainly rode upon strong transnational, anticapitalist themes, but it is fair to say that the digital revolution of the 1990s took the global dissemination of information and global networking to new levels. Most notable was the use of the internet to build contacts among activists in different countries, fostering a virtual dimension to the fundamental network basis of social movements, and raising issues about the nature of transnational social movements that activists and scholars ponder to this day.

At the cutting edge of the trend was the Zapatista movement in Mexico (the EZLN, or Ejército Zapatista de Liberación Nacional) and its international supporters who used the internet in creative ways to pursue "solidarity activism" in support of the movement. The Zapatistas gained international media attention when armed insurgents – mostly Mayan peasants in the Mexican state of Chiapas – seized the capital, San Cristóbal de las Casas, and several other surrounding municipalities on January 1, 1994, the day that NAFTA (the North American Free Trade Agreement) went into effect. The Zapatistas' 11 basic demands were mostly nationally focused (among them employment, land, housing, adequate food and health care, democracy), but because many of these issues intersected with the global justice movement's critiques of free trade and IMF – World Bank structural-adjustment policies, they attracted the attention of a growing cadre of activists in the West, some of whom were highly web-savvy (Bob 2005).

The Zapatistas' internet presence led some researchers to misconstrue the movement as high-tech. Others have noted that the international solidarity generated by internet-based communiqués had great effect in mitigating the Mexican government's reaction and encouraging a peaceful resolution. In fact, however, the Zapatistas were mostly rural and marginalized farmers. Tales of its leaders – especially mediagenic Subcomandante Marcos in his pickup truck with balaclava and pipe – uploading messages to the EZLN website from their laptops were probably wishful high-tech romanticizations of the movement. Olesen (2005) has noted that the vast majority of the Zapatistas' internet postings were done by *international solidarity activists* – supporters mostly in North

American and European countries – not Zapatista leaders. These people regularly reviewed newspaper reports in the Mexican press, notably *La Jornada* (which went online in 1995) to bring the movement's communiqués, press releases, and "denunciations" to the worldwide web (Cleaver 1998). Although some analysts may have overestimated the internet strategy of the EZLN, most correctly saw how the digital battle was over information and its diffusion among globally networked activists and organizations. Cleaver (1998) called this information dimension "a new fabric of struggle."

At the same time, the global justice movement against IMF and G8 policies in poor countries similarly mobilized transnational solidarity networks using internet-based linkages. Throughout the 1990s, protests occurred in cities where IMF, WTO, World Bank, G8, EU, and WEF (World Economic Forum) summits were held: Munich (1992), Lyon (1996), Vancouver (1997), and huge mobilizations in Amsterdam (1997), Luxemburg (1997), Birmingham (1998), Seattle (1999), and Cologne (1999). It is fair to say that the large numbers in the later years reflected not only the mounting criticisms of neoliberal globalization but also the expanding use of temporary websites and listservs to create "computer-supported social networks" (Wellman 2001) as the basis for organizing. Especially notable, and used with great effect during the Seattle protests, independent media centers – Indymedia – were set up as means by which activists shared and collectively produced and edited online text files for international diffusion, and uploaded audio and video images almost in real-time as they occurred. During protests, "media activists" (Juris 2005: 201) used digital cameras (and later their smart phones) to take photos and videos of protests, record police responses, and do interviews with participants in the streets. Downloaded at Indymedia centers, this information was transmitted for real-time updates of the protests around the world. This worldwide connectivity is a key element of the global justice movement. It has given rise to a new organizational form for movement mobilization: geographically dispersed, internet-based global networks, such as Peoples' Global Action, which have no formal members but serve as umbrella spaces for open discussion and exchanges of information on local actions around the world (Juris 2005).

Alterglobalization

Out of the global justice movement emerge several different ideological themes that refocus its antineoliberal critique to explore new possibilities for an interconnected and globalized world. The key idea is that "another world is possible" (hence, *alter*-global), referring to a world *not* based on global corporations, profit seeking, and undemocratic tendencies of powerful economic and political institutions, but rather a world that is radically democratic, progressive, and diversity-affirming. Creating this new world is the guiding concept behind the World Social Forums, large periodic gatherings that lie at the heart of the alterglobalization movement. The forums are partly prefigurative free spaces, partly conferences, partly brainstorming sessions of leftists and antiestablishmentarians, partly demonstrations, and partly celebrations of diversity. In addition to all of these, and as an extension of the trend to transnational activist networks, the forums are opportunities to connect for independent attendees and organizational representatives who share egalitarian and – it has to be said – vaguely defined and highly diverse visions of a different global future.

Main sectors of the movement continue to challenge the economic and cultural globalization advocated by the world's richest states, as well as the production and investment practices that foster economic injustices. Yet it is fair to say that a parallel theme of the movement is the creation of a positive, alternative democratic space to counter the elitist and undemocratic forces that lie behind global trends. This theme gathered momentum during the anti-IMF protests in the 1990s, and reached its apex shortly after the new millennium. The first Social Forum took place in Porto Alegre, Brazil, in January 2001. A second forum was held in Mumbai in 2004, and a third returned to Brazil in 2005. Regional Social Forums have been organized in numerous other settings, especially in Europe and Latin America. European Social Forums were held in Florence (2002), Paris (2003), and London (2004), and a US Social Forum in Atlanta (2007). Participants consider these gatherings to be expressions of an emerging *global civil society* (see Smith and Reese 2008).

Two threads that are woven in the theme of creating a new democratic space are: (1) a conscious emphasis on maintaining diversity, equality, and broad participation in decision making, such that the pursuit of single ideological platforms and political agendas are usually rejected; and (2) a collective recognition that the "process is the purpose." This refers to how the practices that the gatherings employ to organize and act reflect a radical vision of democratic equality. The line of descent of these organizational and decision-making practices goes back to some movements of the late 1960s and early 1970s, and their emphasis on consensus decision making, which contrasted to the Old Left's hierarchical structures (Breines 1980, 1982). Then feminist collectives, peace organizations, antinuclear and environmental groups carried the torch of participatory democratic decision-making practices during the 1980s and 1990s, passing it to activists in the antineoliberal globalization movement, where it found further elaboration in the *encuentros* of the Zapatistas and then the alterglobalization movement (Maeckelbergh 2011).

Drawing on della Porta (2009: 185) the main principles of participatory democracy can be summed up as follows: (1) decisions are taken by consensus; (2) they require public engagement of differing points of view, yielding (3) the transformation of different perspectives through rational argument; (4) everyone with a stake in the topics being discussed has a right to participate in the decision making; (5) deliberation is among equals, meaning all participants are respected by giving them an equal chance to influence discussion. Researchers have noted that, in practice, these principles often cause frustration and conflict (Polletta 2002; Juris 2008; Kwon, Reese, and Anantran 2008; della Porta 2009), yet they also note that strong commitment, idealism, and hope among its participants (Pleyers 2011; Smith and Reese 2008; Smith 2008) – in large part sustained by shared values of equality, diversity, economic justice, and tolerance – in addition to a faith in the wisdom of the popular will channeled these "horizontal" democratic principles.

Tarrow (2005: 73) observes that, under the umbrella of the movement, an extraordinary breadth of issues are included: "opponents of free trade, supporters of a cleaner environment, those who demand access for third-world farmers to Western markets, opponents of neoliberalism, and supporters of global democracy." In addition to these themes, we can add internet freedom and cyberactivism. Juris (2005: 204) discusses one group called d.sec (for database systems to enforce control), a cyberactivist group at an alterglobal encampment in Germany. In their own words, the group is:

> An open structure where activists, anti-racists, migrants, hackers, techs, artists and many more put their knowledge and practices into self-organized interaction: a space to discuss and network, skill share, and produce collaborative knowledge. A laboratory to try out ways to hack the streets and reclaim cyberspace with crowds in pink and silver; experiment with virtual identities, Linux, and open source . . . explore the embodiment of technology, learn about the meanings of physical and virtual border crossing.

Obviously, there is a strong techie orientation in this group's activities, but they are solidly embedded in the alterglobalization ethos insofar as open and free digital access lies at the heart of the movement's global communication network and participatory democratic goals. As their flyer states, activists, antiracists, migrants, hackers, and artists are all welcome to their big tent.

Process Tactics and Site Occupations

The processes of participatory democracy, inspired by a different set of demands, have been expropriated recently by movements occurring in mostly national contexts. I have in mind the Occupy movements (the 2011 occupation of Wall Street and numerous other central districts in cities in the US and throughout the world) and, their precursor by several months, the *Indignados* (the indignant ones) movement in Spain, which also occupied central plazas of major Spanish cities with *acampadas* (encampments). The *acampadas* in Barcelona and Madrid were the central sites of the movement, also called 15-M (for May 15, 2011, when the occupations began). The impetus for these movements was outrage at the economic inequalities in the wake of the 2008 financial crisis and how these inequalities fell disproportionately on the generation of 18- to 30-year-olds. But in addition to these claims, the occupations created spaces where intensely experienced collective identities were forged for participants, based on local cultures of diversity and, above all, collective participation in "methodologies" for consensus democracy among mostly young-generation occupiers.

Looking back on these movements, both seem to have faded away. Neither was able to rekindle initial enthusiasm on their one-year anniversaries, nor did they maintain widespread activism once their occupations were dispersed. However, the tactic of site occupations as prefigurative free spaces – that is, visions of a possible future – has not disappeared, and there is evidence that it is becoming an established element of the modern repertoire. Two years after the Wall Street encampment, an occupation of Taksim Square in Istanbul, Turkey, was begun by mostly young protesters. Their claims were diverse, ranging from protecting the square from a planned shopping mall to halting the encroaching authoritarianism of the ruling Justice and Development Party, a conservative Islamic party in Turkey; but the tactics of consensus democracy and identity affirmation were similar (Arsu and Yeginsu 2013). Participants from Occupy Wall Street would immediately recognize the yoga classes, law centers, medical tents, community gardens, intense discussions, and the tent encampments among the occupiers. Interestingly, there was a small presence of transnational activists, which is why Prime Minister Recep Tayyip Erdogan blamed foreign agitators for the unrest.

Of course, sit-ins and factory occupations are time-tested protest tactics. However, these recent occupations are distinguished by: (1) the absence of extensive formal planning, with short-term and instantaneous digital communication in its place; (2) diversity among participants; and (3) compared to the mobilizing structures of the civil rights movement or women's movement, relative anonymity among those present, at least at the outset of the encampments. These qualities contrast with their more traditional close cousins – say, occupations of university buildings, where established campus groups initiate the actions, or with sit-ins and/or work slowdowns at factories called for by local unions. In these cases, participants know each other beforehand. Nor do these older tactics capture the celebratory, innovative, and new-identity-building qualities of the occupations.

The trend line for this new species of occupation goes back in part to the first camps that sprang up around the anti-IMF and anti-G8 protests of the 1990s. Also, Soule (1997) has traced the early diffusion of the encampment tactics in the form of student-occupied shantytowns to protest against university investment strategies. These lines were further developed through the Zapatista *encuentros* and the Social Forums of the alterglobalization movement. But also woven into these actions is a cultural thread that was first spun by the NSMs of the early 1980s – feminism, environmentalism, gay rights, and so on – such that concrete claims of injustice are merged with processes of identity formation, affirmation, and lifestyle definition. Although digital communication is a factor present in all these encampments – and here is the punch line – the end point in all cases is the intense face-to-face experience of new personal encounters, not virtual ones. Maeckelbergh's participant-observation description of these occupations (2011: 209) stressed the open-door nature of the occupations, and the personal contacts among networked transnational activists. Other research chronicles the intense sense of community created in them (Smith 2008; Smith and Reese 2008; Pleyers 2011). Moreover, the intense participatory focus of the occupations can dilute the original demands of the gathering. This dilution is often compounded by the broad diversity of claims and grievances – embraced as part of the process itself – that decreases singular emphasis on any one of them and amplifies the process dimension even more.

Site occupations are a new "process tactic" fueled by the strong solidary incentives experienced by those who take part in democratic deliberation and consensus building, much like the identity-building processes of NSMs discussed in chapter 4. In the NSMs of the past, there were always some groups whose emphasis diverted energies away from social-change goals in favor of personal change. But, also, those NSMs had networked organizational structures that endured beyond these specific settings of "identity work," such as small groups and discussion circles. In contrast, alterglobalization and encampment mobilizations create collective-identity experiences in large temporary gatherings that form and disperse with – as the evidence suggests so far – only weak and lingering structures to give continuity to their policy claims. It may be that if process tactics over-shadow outcomes as mobilization goals of future campaigns, movements like alterglobalization and the Occupy encampments augur a future of identity and lifestyle movements of a different kind, propagating temporary forms of solidarity as digital communication and social media bring diverse populations together quickly.

Social Movements and Contemporary Society

To conclude our assessment of trends and to underline the significance of our field of study in general, I would like to close by proposing that social movements are playing an increasingly important role in contemporary politics and society (Goldstone 2003). As the examples I have just discussed indicate, this is occurring in both democracies and autocratic regimes. This means that social movement research increasingly captures central trends in modern society and draws the discipline to the core of social science theorizing about the shape of the postmodern world. Simply stated, social movements and protest mobilization are key processes in the contemporary world, and understanding them and their relation to governance and policy tells us a lot about how societies cohere and change. I would go as far as saying that the growth of the field since the 1970s reflects these trends. Today, the sections of social movement research are among the largest in both the American Sociological Association and the International Sociological Association, the most important professional groups for sociologists, but, as recently as the 1970s, these sections did not exist at all. It is not hubris to say that this reflects the growing importance of the field of study.

Regarding the Western democracies, Meyer and Tarrow (1998) introduced the term *social movement society* to capture how movements are becoming more common as a means to express political claims. Melucci (1989) used the label *the movementization of society* to describe similar processes, but he laid emphasis on networks of social affiliation that permeate the contemporary urban landscape and how these are the basis of new and complex collective identities. Other researchers have explored the various dimensions of the trend – frequency, size, tactics (Dalton 2002; Dodson 2011; Rucht 1999; Soule and Earl 2005) – with the general conclusion that, although the jury is out about whether protests are simply more frequent than before, it is fair to say that social movement tactics are more widely accepted as a means to express demands and/or grievances. Moreover, as the discussion in the preceding section suggests, new forms of collective action are emerging to perform other social functions, such as imagining future social relations, which only works to increase the incidence of social movement activity even more.

One way to approach the social movement society thesis is to ask the basic question "Are protests and demonstrations becoming more frequent?" Rucht (1998) looked at newspaper reports of protest events to find that, between 1950 and 1992, there was an overall increase in protest actions in West Germany, especially nonviolent and nonconfrontational kinds such as demonstrations, marches, rallies, and so on. He also found that the size of protests grew during the period. Soule and Earl's (2005) examination of over 19,000 newspaper reports of US protest events between 1960 and 1986 similarly found that the size of protests had increased, but their data did not show a clear upward trend in number of events, but rather peaks and valleys. They found a strong organizing presence of SMOs in protest events, and that over time, SMOs concentrated, a finding that suggests that they were becoming larger and more efficient. It is entirely plausible that the increased role of larger SMOs is because they are better able to get their messages out and market them more effectively. On the other hand, because new digital technologies greatly facilitate the coordination of protest campaigns and actions, they may counterbalance this trend in the long term. These are important research questions that need to be addressed.

A related question is whether more people are participating in social movements. Dodson (2011), using data based on individuals' self-reports, finds that in 18 advanced Western democracies, this indeed seems to be the trend. This is supported by Dalton's earlier survey research (2002), which reported that more Americans participated in protest actions than ever before, and that this number has increased significantly over the past several decades. Over 25 percent of his respondents report having taken part in a protest action. Increased protest participation may be due to decreased risk. Several studies suggest that more peaceable forms of claims making have increased while highly contentious and/or violent forms have not (Everett 1992; Kriesi 1995; Meyer and Tarrow 1998). Softer police tactics in controlling protests also have much to do with this. Soule and Earl's (2005) US study shows that, since 1967, there has been a steady decline in property damage and violence in protests. That year, 33 percent of protests were violent and 21 percent involved property damage. By 1986, less than 10 percent of protests were violent and 2 percent led to property damage. All these trends indicate how the field of social movement research focuses on an increasingly important element of modern society: collective action as a common means of voicing group demands, which, in turn, is central to democratic governance.

Another way to think about these trends is that they fall under the broader category of the *institutionalization* of the social movement repertoire. This has two streams: (1) tactics and forms of organization characteristic of protest movements are used by more established groups and organizations – with the tendency that they protest more peaceably and with more decorum; and (2) social movement groups are becoming more bureaucratized, professionalized, and institutionalized.

Regarding the first point, interest groups, advocacy organizations, and political action committees that pursue social change agendas have increased in numbers significantly since the 1960s. Organizations evolved out of the major movements of the period to establish themselves as political players, especially the major organizations of the civil rights and women's movements (Minkoff 1995). Later, the process was further encouraged in the US by the post-Watergate political reforms (Knoke 1986). While interest groups and NGOs mostly pursue their claims through established institutional channels such as grant writing, lobbying, advising legislation, press releases, and public relations campaigns, evidence suggests that they increasingly employ noninstitutional means to spread their messages, such as rallies, demonstrations, petition campaigns, and protests (Minkoff 1994; Walker 1991).

Such tactics help to attract media attention and influence public opinion. In the growing marketplace of competing change-oriented groups, dramatic demonstrations are more visible and more newsworthy. Using them is a strategic decision that must be balanced between forcefulness (to get the attention) and moderation (so that they will be taken seriously). The entry of highly effective, highly organized, mostly non-movement groups into the protest arena tends to marginalize resource-poor movement groups and factions holding more extreme ideological stances. These groups may consider disruption and even violence as the only way their voice can be heard. This helps to explain an apparent paradox in several Western democracies that, although more and more moderate groups are protesting politely, there is the persistence of small, violent actions, such as abortion clinic bombings, fires set by Earth Liberation Front militants, and the destruction of testing laboratories by the Animal Liberation Front. Dodson's findings (2011) seem to confirm this. He has found this mix of tactics is the trend in several advanced Western countries.

The study of political parties is a central focus of research in political science, and there has traditionally been a line of demarcation between political-party research (as institutional politics) and the field of social movements (which studies *transgressive* politics). However the normalization of movement tactics is clearly seen in the Tea Party movement in the US, which gathered strength after the election of President Obama in 2008 (Meyer and Van Dyke 2014). The Tea Party uses the tactics and local organizational models of social movements, and functions as a movement within the Republican Party to call attention to issues that are not represented in the party's platform. It mixes mainstream political tactics such as meetings, canvassing, and participating in state party organizations and social movement tactics such as rallies and public protests. Tea Party organizations in various states have held demonstrations, town-hall meetings, and campaigns to put pressure on Republican Party organizations to adapt small-government, antitax, and libertarian platforms. Often, they offer their own candidates in Republican primary elections. They sometimes mobilize protests against the policies of the Democrats, especially regarding taxes, health care, or immigration issues, or they may hold protests at appearances of opposing politicians. Conflicts and schisms within parties and organizations are not new phenomena, but the use of movement campaign tactics – rather than (or in addition to) in-fighting among cliques and/or negotiations within an organization or party – is a more recent development that further suggests the institutionalization trend.

Regarding the second stream of this trend, the professionalization of the social movement sector is a pattern that is not likely to disappear in the near future. Change-oriented NGOs and large SMOs are staffed by full-time social movement professionals who often bring training in organizing, management, and fundraising to their organizations. These organizations have a complex division of labor and authority, which makes them more efficient in strategizing goals and implementing campaigns. Marketing, grant writing, and checkbook memberships have become key themes of large professionalized SMOs. Money brings power and stability to these organizations, which permits them to assert a more consistent presence in the political system compared to smaller SMOs.

On the one hand, this trend can be seen as a positive development because expanding the social movement sector opens more channels of influence for citizens and increases democratic participation. Movement pressure can make politicians and decision makers more responsive to citizen demands, and mitigate tendencies that concentrate power in organs of government. On the other hand, these same oligarchic tendencies paradoxically are often at work within the professionalized organizations, producing a counterforce that decreases internal democratic participation. Social movement professionals may make decisions themselves on the basis of efficiency, timeliness, and skills. Piven and Cloward's study of poor people's movements showed that centralized decision making limits grassroots inputs and decreases the likelihood of disruptive protest while increasing the likelihood of cooptation and compromise of the movement's demands (Piven and Cloward 1977; see also Piven 2012)

The question is whether large SMOs can keep their contentious mojo in the face of professionalization. They may have to work very hard at it, as a recent "direct action" by Greenpeace demonstrates. At a reception recently held by Shell to showcase the new offshore drilling operations in the Arctic Ocean, the guest list was infiltrated by activists posing as industry personnel. They rigged a huge ice sculpture of the Shell logo to spew a dark liquid (really Diet Coke) over the guests. An elderly woman (also an activist) was hit directly and shrieked in horror as other activists video-recorded it all to post it on YouTube. The next day Greenpeace activists took calls from reporters to explain the drama as a Twitter feed was projected on the wall behind them (Murphy 2012). Reporters were the prank's target, not Shell executives or policymakers, and the goal was media exposure to raise awareness of Shell's plans. Such staged actions are not new to Greenpeace, but the example – a combination of web-based diffusion of the action, media strategy, and dramatic creativity in the action's conception – may offer a hint of future variations in the professionalized social movement repertoire.

However, I close by juxtaposing this example with the cases of real and authentic popular mobilization in the Occupy Wall Street, M-15, and Taksim Square (in Turkey) mobilizations discussed earlier. In these cases, the participation occurred without SMO professional strategizing, and protests took on a life of their own via the face-to-face experiences of the occupations. The emerging power of social media and digital communication technologies greatly facilitated coordination and mobilization functions, first in the initial calls to participate and then in the coordination of on-the-ground protests. In all cases, the main goal and the raison d'être of the calls to mobilize were the face-to-face gatherings – not virtual in the least – as expressions of collective grievances. The real-time sharing of the experience of collective action is – and will remain – the fundamental element in the social movement repertoire because it is through the claims and demands of large popular protests that politicians gauge shifts in public opinion, and that the public expresses its limits of tolerance and aspirations for the future. But also, collective gatherings are emotionally charged sites where participants develop a shared sense of time, place, and common purpose that is central to the protest experience, and common identities. This too is a reason for the persistence of protest tactics, despite digital alternatives.

A case in point is that, in June and July 2013, the huge demonstrations occurred in Brazil, initiated by the powerful use of Twitter, mobile phones, blogs, Facebook, and Bluetooth. These were the largest demonstrations in Brazil since the mid-1980s, initiated mostly by students and youth. One estimate places the size of the protests in Rio de Janeiro at 100,000 people, and 65,000 in São Paulo. Protests mobilized quickly in 100 Brazilian cities. In the words of one Brazilian researcher, they were distinguished "by refusal to be defined by one single objective and by the extensive use of social media, which enabled them to evolve fast in response to various sources of social and political tension in Brazil" (Romero 2013a).

Protests were precipitated by what might appear to be a minor grievance, anger at fare increases on public transportation, but they quickly refocused on broader issues such as corruption, unresponsiveness and ineptitude in the government, and budget priorities, as they had in the Egyptian and Tunisian Revolutions, and in the Turkish occupations. It is interesting that Brazil's president, once an antigovernment militant herself, who, years ago, fought against Brazil's dictatorship, said she was "proud of the protesters": "These voices, which go beyond traditional mechanisms – political parties and the media itself – need to be heard. . . . The magnitude of the demonstrations is proof of the energy of our democracy" (Romero 2013b). Although her statement is no doubt partly political spin, from our perspective on the field of study, she got it right. In the twenty-first century, social movements are an integral part of functioning democracies because democratic regimes often do not function very well.

In North America and Europe, these protests will have faded into obscurity by the time you read these words, but the general point is lasting: social movements are key elements of how politics is accomplished in modern society. But not only that: as we saw in the Arab Spring mobilizations, they also are key sources of political change when state systems are repressive, unresponsive, and ossified. And also, as we saw in the Occupy Wall Street and M-15 mobilizations, and the World Social Forums, they can be key sources of broader social change, of new social relations, and for rethinking possible futures in creative and innovative ways. Face-to-face, real-time, collective action in the form of seizing the streets and central plazas will never be replaced. This, I propose, is reflected in the celebratory and identity-affirming characteristics of several recent movements that protest a broad array of grievances against politics-as-usual: the Occupy movements (2011), the Brazilian movement (2013), the Israeli protests against living costs (2011), Greek and Irish protests about austerity (2008–13), Indian protests over corruption (2011), Chilean student protests (2011–12), and the Turkish protests against the ruling party's social conservatism (2013). These were all huge mobilizations, and digital technologies point to more and more of them on more and more different and diverse issues, with more and more people mobilized more and more quickly – at least these are hypotheses for social movement researchers to ponder. And do these mobilizations keep democracies responsive? The short answer is "Yes." They are integral to keeping political elites attentive. When you close this book, go online to the major news services and see where social movements are occurring right now. Not only in terms of research and scholarship, where new technologies permit rapid analysis of digital communications among protesters, but also in terms of broad sweeps of social change and the processes of democratic responsiveness, all these developments suggest it is an exciting time to be studying social movements.

References

Abeles, Ronald P. 1976. "Relative Deprivation, Rising Expectations and Black Militancy." *Journal of Social Issues* 32: 119–37.

Alexander, Jeffery C. 2011. *Performative Revolution in Egypt: An Essay in Cultural Power*. London: Bloomsbury Academic.

Alexander, Jeffrey C., and Jason L. Mast. 2006. "Symbolic Action in Theory and Practice: The Cultural Pragmatics of Symbolic Action." pp. 1–28 in *Social Performance: Symbolic Action, Cultural Pragmatics, and Ritual*, edited by Jeffrey C. Alexander, Bernhard Geisen, and Jason L. Mast. New York: Cambridge University Press.

Almeida, Paul. 2008. *Waves of Protest: Popular Struggle in El Salvador, 1925–2005*. Minneapolis: University of Minnesota Press.

Alreck, Pamela L., and Robert B. Settle. 2004. *The Survey Research Handbook*. Third edition. New York: McGraw Hill / Irwin.

Amenta, Edwin, and Yvonne Zylan. 1991. "It Happened Here: Political Opportunity, the New Institutionalism, and the Townsend Movement." *American Sociological Review* 56: 250–65.

Arendt, Hannah. 1951. *The Origins of Totalitarianism*. New York: Harcourt Brace.

Arsu, Sebnem, and Ceylan Yeginsu. 2013. "Turkish Leader Offers Referendum on Park at Center of Protests." *New York Times*, June 13: A8.

Arthur, Mikaila Mariel Lemonik. 2011. *Student Activism and Curricular Change in Higher Education*. Farnham: Ashgate.

Austin Holmes, Amy. 2012. "There are Weeks When Decades Happen: Structure and Strategy in the Egyptian Revolution." *Mobilization: An International Quarterly* 17: 391–410.

Babbie, Earl R. 1990. *Survey Research Methods*. Second edition. Belmont, CA: Wadsworth.

Barranco, José, and Dominique Wisler. 1999. "Validity and Systematicity of Newspaper Data in Event Analysis." *European Sociological Review* 15: 301–22.

Beissinger, Mark R. 2002. *Nationalist Mobilization and the Collapse of the Soviet State*. New York: Cambridge University Press.

Bernstein, Mary 1997. "Celebration and Suppression: The Strategic Uses of Identity by the Lesbian and Gay Movement." *American Journal of Sociology* 103: 537–65.

Billig, Michael. 1992. *Talking of the Royal Family*. London: Routledge.

Billig, Michael. 1995. "Rhetorical Psychology, Ideological Thinking, and Imaging Nationhood." pp. 64–81 in *Social Movements and Culture*, edited by Hank Johnston and Bert Klandermans. Minneapolis: University of Minnesota Press.

Blee, Kathleen M. 1991. *Women of the Klan: Racism and Gender in the 1920s*. Berkeley: University of California Press.

Blee, Kathleen M., and Verta Taylor. 2002. "Semi-Structured Interviewing in Social Movement Research." pp. 92–117 in *Methods of Social Movement Research*, edited by Bert Klandermans and Susan Staggenborg. Minneapolis: University of Minnesota Press.

Blumer, Herbert. 1951 "Collective Behavior." pp. 167–222 in *A New Outline of the Principles of Sociology*, edited by A. McClung Lee. New York: Barnes and Noble.

Bob, Clifford. 2005. *The Marketing of Rebellion*. New York: Cambridge University Press.

Bond, Doug, J. Craig Jenkins, Charles L. Taylor, and Kurt Schock. 1997. "Mapping Mass Political Conflict and Civil Society: The Automated Development of Event Data." *Journal of Conflict Resolution* 41: 553–79.

Bosi, Lorenzo, Chares Demitriou, and Stefan Malthaner. 2014. *The Dynamics of Radicalization: A Processual Perspective*. Farnham: Ashgate.

Breines, Wini. 1980. "Community and Organization: The New Left and Michels' 'Iron Law.'" *Social Problems* 27(4): 419–29.

Breines, Wini. 1982. *Community and Organization in the New Left*. South Hadley, MA: J. F. Bergin.

Bruce, Tricia Coleen. 2011. *Faithful Revolution: How Voice of the Faithful Is Changing the Church*. New York: Oxford University Press.

Buechler, Stephen. 2000. *Social Movements in Advanced Capitalism: The Political Economy and Cultural Construction of Activism*. New York: Oxford University Press.

Casquette, Jesus. 1996. "The Sociopolitical Context of Mobilization: The Case of the Antimilitary Movement in the Basque Country." *Mobilization: An International Quarterly* 1: 203–20.

Castells, Manuel. 1996. *The Rise of the Networked Society*. Malden, MA: Blackwell.

Castells, Manuel. 1997. *The Power of Identity*. Malden, MA: Blackwell.

Chabot, Sean. 2000. "Transnational Diffusion and the African-American Reinvention of the Gandhian Repertoire." *Mobilization: An International Quarterly* 5: 201–16.

Cleaver, Jr., H. M. 1998. "The Zapatista Effect: The Internet and the Rise of an Alternative Political Fabric." *Journal of International Affairs* 51: 2.

Clemens, Elisabeth S. 1997. *The Peoples Lobby: Organizational Innovation and the Rise of Interest Groups in the United States, 1890–1925*. Chicago: University of Chicago Press.

Clemens, Elisabeth S., and Martin D. Hughes. 2002. "Recovering Past Protest: Historical Research on Social Movements." pp. 201–30 in *Methods of Social Movement Research*, edited by Bert Klandermans and Susan Staggenborg. Minneapolis: University of Minnesota Press.

Dalton, Russell J. 1994. *The Green Rainbow: Environmental Groups in Western Europe*. New Haven, CT: Yale University Press.

Dalton, Russell. 2002. *Citizen Politics: Public Opinion and Political Parties in Advanced Industrial Democracies*. Third Edition. New York: Chatham House Publishers.

Davies, James. 1969. "The J-Curve of Rising and Declining Satisfactions as Cause of Some Great Revolutions and a Contained Rebellion." pp. 690–730 in *Violence in America*, edited by H. D. Graham and Ted Robert Gurr. New York: Praeger.

De Fazio, Gianluca. 2013. "The Radicalization of Contention in Northern Ireland, 1968–1972: A Relational Perspective." *Mobilization* 18: 457–75.

della Porta, Donatella. 1992. "Life History Analysis of Activists." pp. 168–93 in *Studying Collective Action*, edited by Mario Diani and Ron Eyerman. London: Sage.

della Porta, Donatella. 2002. "Comparative Politics and Social Movements." pp. 286–313 in *Methods of Social Movement Research*, edited by Bert Klandermans and Susan Staggenborg. Minneapolis: University of Minnesota Press.

della Porta, Donatella. 2009. "Making the New Polis: The Practice of Deliberative Democracy in Social Forums." pp. 181–208 in *Culture, Social Movements and Protest*, edited by Hank Johnston. Farnham: Ashgate.

della Porta, Donatella, and Mario Diani. 2006. *Social Movements: An Introduction*. Second edition. Malden, MA: Blackwell Publishing.

DeNardo, James. 1985. *Power in Numbers: The Political Strategy of Protest and Rebellion*. Princeton, NJ: Princeton University Press.

Denisoff, R. Serge, and Richard Peterson. 1973. *The Sounds of Social Change*. New York: Rand McNally.

Diani, Mario. 1992. "The Concept of Social Movement." *Sociological Review* 40: 1–25.

Diani, Mario. 1995. *Green Networks: A Structural Analysis of the Italian Environmental Movement*. Edinburgh: Edinburgh University Press.

Diani, Mario. 1996. "Linking Mobilization Frames and Political Opportunities: Insights from Regional Populism in Italy." *American Sociological Review* 61: 1053–69.

Diani, Mario. 2002. "Network Analysis." pp. 173–200 in *Methods of Social Movement Research*, edited by Bert Klandermans and Susan Staggenborg. Minneapolis: University of Minnesota Press.

Diani, Mario, and Doug McAdam, eds. 2003. *Social Movement Networks*. New York: Oxford University Press.

Dodson, Kyle. 2011. "The Movement Society in Comparative Perspective." *Mobilization: An International Quarterly* 16: 475–94.

Duncombe, Stephen. 1997. *Notes from the Underground: Zines and the Politics of Alternative Culture*. New York: Verso.

Earl, Jennifer, and Katrina Kimport. 2011. *Digitally Enabled Social Change*. Cambridge, MA: MIT Press.

Eisinger, Peter K. 1973. "The Conditions of Protest Behavior in American Cities." *American Political Science Review* 67: 11–28.

Erikson, Eric. 1968. *Identity: Youth and Crisis*. New York: Norton.

Everett, Kevin. D. 1992. "Professionalization and Protest: Changes in the Social Movement Sector, 1961–1983." *Social Forces* 70: 957–75.

Eyerman, Ron. 2006. "Performing Opposition, or How Social Movements Move." pp. 193–217 in *Social Performance: Symbolic Action, Cultural Pragmatics and Ritual*, edited by Jeffrey Alexander, Bernhard Giesen, and Jason L. Mast. New York: Cambridge University Press.

Eyerman, Ron, and Andrew Jamison. 1998. *Music and Social Movements*. New York: Cambridge University Press.

Flam, Helena, and Debra King, eds. 2005. *Emotions and Social Movements*. New York: Routledge.

Fowler, Floyd. 2009. *Survey Research Methods*, Fourth edition. Thousand Oaks, CA: Sage.

Franzosi, Roberto. 2004. *From Words to Numbers: Narrative, Data, and Social Science*. Cambridge: Cambridge University Press.

Franzosi, Roberto. 2010. *Quantitative Narrative Analysis*. Los Angeles: Sage.

Frazier, E. Franklin. 1963. *The Negro Church in America*. New York: Schocken Books.

Gamson, William A. 1989. "Media Discourse and Public Opinion on Nuclear Power: A Constructionist Approach." *American Journal of Sociology* 95: 1–37.

Gamson, William. 1990 [1975]. *The Strategy of Social Protest*. Second edition. Belmont, CA: Wadsworth.

Gamson, William A. 1992a. *Talking Politics*. New York: Cambridge University Press.

Gamson, William. 1992b. "The Social Psychology of Collective Action." pp. 53–76 in *Frontiers of Social Movement Theory*, edited by Aldon Morris and Carol McClurg Mueller. New Haven, CT: Yale University Press.

Gamson, William. 2004a. "On a Sociology of the Media." *Political Communication* 21: 305–27.

Gamson, William. 2004b. "Bystanders, Public Opinion, and the Media." pp. 242–61 in *Blackwell Companion to Social Movements*, edited by David Snow, Sarah Soule, and Hanspeter Kreisi. Malden, MA: Blackwell.

Gamson, William, and David S. Meyer. 1996. "Framing Political Opportunity." pp. 275–90 in *Comparative Perspectives on Social Movements: Political Opportunities, Mobilizing Structures, and Cultural Framings*, edited by Doug McAdam, John D. McCarthy, and Mayer N. Zald. New York: Cambridge University Press.

Gamson, William A., and Gadi Wolsfeld. 1993. "Movements and Media as Interacting Systems." *Annals of the American Academy of Political and Social Science* 528: 114–25.

Gamson, William A., Bruce Fireman, and Steven Rytina. 1982. *Encounters with Unjust Authority*. Homewood, IL: Dorsey Press.

Gans, Herbert J. 1979. *Deciding What's News: A Study of CBS Evening News, NBC Nightly News, Newsweek, and Time*. New York: Pantheon Books.

Geddes, Barbara. 1999. "What Do We Know about Democratization after Twenty Years?" *Annual Review of Political Science* 2: 115–44.

Gerlach, Luther, and Virgina Hine. 1970. *People, Power, and Change*. Indianapolis, IN: Bobbs-Merrill.

Geshwender, James A. 1964. "Social Structure and the Negro Revolt: An Examination of Some Hypotheses." *Social Forces* 43: 248–56.

Gitlin, Todd. 1980. *The Whole World Is Watching: Mass Media in the Making and Unmaking of the New Left*. Berkeley: University of California Press.

Givan, Rebecca Kolins, Kenneth. M. Roberts, and Sarah A. Soule. 2010. "Introduction: The Dimensions of Diffusion." Pp. 1–20 in *The Diffusion of Social Movements: Actors, Mechanisms, and Political Effects*, edited by R. K. Given, K. M. Roberts, and Sarah A. Soule. New York: Cambridge University Press.

Goldfarb, Jeffrey. 1980. *The Persistence of Freedom*. Boulder, CO: Westview Press.

Goldstone, Jack. 2003. "Introduction: Bridging Institutionalized and Noninstitutionalized Politics." pp. 1–25 in *States, Parties, and Social Movements*, edited by Jack Goldstone. New York: Cambridge University Press.

Goldstone, Jack, and Charles Tilly. 2001. "Threat (and Opportunity): Popular Action and State Response in the Dynamics of Contentious Action." pp. 179–94 in *Silence and Voice in the Study of Contentious Politics*, edited by Ronald Aminzade, Jack A. Goldstone, Doug McAdam, et al. New York: Cambridge University Press.

Goodwin, Jeff, and James M. Jasper. 2004. "Caught in a Winding, Snarling Vine: The Structural Bias of Political Process Theory." pp. 3–30 in *Rethinking Social Movement: Structure, Meaning, and Emotions*, edited by Jeff Goodwin and James J. Jasper. Lanham, MD: Rowman & Littlefield.

Goodwin, Jeffery, James Jasper, and Francesca Polletta. 2001. "Why Emotions Matter." Pp. 1–24 in *Passionate Politics*, edited by Jeff Goodwin, James Jasper, and Francesca Polletta. Chicago: University of Chicago Press.

Goodwin, Jeff, James M. Jasper, and Francesca Polletta. 2004. "Emotional Dimensions of Social Movements." pp. 413–32 in *The Blackwell Companion to Social Movements*, edited by David Snow, Sarah Soule, and Hanspeter Kriesi. Malden, MA: Blackwell.

Gould, Deborah. 2002. "Life During Wartime: Emotions and the Development of ACT-UP." *Mobilization* 7: 177–200.

Gould, Deborah. 2009. *Moving Politics: Emotion and ACT UP's Fight Against AIDS*. Chicago: University of Chicago Press.

Gould, Roger V. 1995. *Insurgent Identities: Class, Community, and Protest in Paris from 1948 to the Commune*. Chicago: University of Chicago Press.

Gurr, Ted Robert. 1970. *Why Men Rebel*. Princeton, NJ: Princeton University Press.

Haenfler, Ross. 2006. *Straight Edge: Clean-Living Youth, Hardcore Punk, and Social Change*. New Brunswick, NJ: Rutgers University Press.

Haines, Herbert. 1988. *Black Radicals and the Civil Rights Mainstream 1954–1970*. Knoxville: University of Tennessee Press.

Halebsky, Stephen. 2006. "Explaining the Outcomes of the Antisuperstore Movement: A Comparative Analysis of Six Communities." *Mobilization: An International Quarterly* 14: 443–61.

Halker, Clark D. 1991. *For Democracy, Workers, and God: Labor Song-Poems and Labor Protest 1865–95*. Urbana: University of Illinois Press.

Hanagan, Michael. 2002. "Irish Transnational Social Movements, Migrants, and the State System." pp. 53–74 in *Globalization and Resistance*, edited by Jackie Smith and Hank Johnston. Lanham, MD: Rowman and Littlefield.

Harding, Timothy. 1969. *Mexico '68: The Students Speak*. New York: US Committee for Justice to Latin American Political Prisoners.

Howard, Phillip N. 2010. *The Digital Origins of Dictatorship and Democracy*. New York: Oxford University Press.

Hug, Simon, and Dominique Wisler. 1998. "Correcting for Selection Bias in Social Movement Research." *Mobilization: An International Quarterly* 3: 141–61.

Hunt, Scott, and Robert Benford. 1994. "Identity Talk in the Peace and Justice Movement." *Journal of Contemporary Ethnography* 22: 488–517.

Jansen, Robert S. 2007. "Resurrection and Appropriation: Reputational Trajectories, Memory Work, and the Political Use of

Historical Figures." *American Journal of Sociology* 112: 953–1007.

Jasper, James. 2012. "Introduction: From Political Opportunity Structures to Strategic Interaction." pp. 1–33 in *Contention in Context*, edited by Jeff Goodwin and James M. Jasper. Stanford, CA: Stanford University Press.

Jenness, Valerie, and Kendall Broad. 1997. *Hate Crimes: New Social Movements and the Politics of Violence*. Hawthorne, NY: Aldine de Gruyter.

Johnston, Hank. 1991. *Tales of Nationalism: Catalonia, 1939–1979*. New Brunswick, NJ: Rutgers University Press.

Johnston, Hank. 1995. "A Methodology for Frame Analysis: From Discourse to Cognitive Schemata." pp. 217–46 in *Social Movements and Culture*, edited by Hank Johnston and Bert Klandermans. Minneapolis: University of Minnesota Press.

Johnston, Hank. 2002. "Verification and Proof in Frame and Discourse Analysis." pp. 62–91 in *Methods of Social Movement Research*, edited by Bert Klandermans and Suzanne Staggenborg. Minneapolis: University of Minnesota Press.

Johnston, Hank. 2006. "Let's Get Small: The Dynamics of (Small) Contention in Repressive States." *Mobilization: An International Quarterly* 11: 195–212.

Johnston, Hank. 2009. *Culture, Social Movements and Protest*. Farnham: Ashgate.

Johnston, Hank, 2010. "Cultural Analysis of Political Protest." pp. 327–47 in *Handbook of Politics*, edited by Kevin T. Leicht and J. Craig Jenkins. New York: Springer.

Johnston, Hank. 2011. *States and Social Movements*. Cambridge: Polity.

Johnston, Hank. 2013. "The Elephant in the Room: Youth, Generational Change, and Cognitive Development in Social Movement Activism." A paper presented at the European Sociological Association Meetings, September 3–5, Turin, Italy.

Johnston, Hank, and Eitan Y. Alimi. 2013. "The Grammar of Frame Dynamics: Analyzing Key Battles in Palestinian Nationalism." *Mobilization* 18: 453–76.

Johnston, Hank, and Cole Carnesecca. 2014. "Fear Management in Contemporary Antiauthoritarian Oppositions." pp. 75–94 in *From Silence to Protest*, edited by Frédéric Royall and Didier Chabanet. Farnham: Ashgate.

Johnston, Hank, and Bert Klandermans. 1995. *Culture and Social Movements*. Minneapolis: University of Minnesota Press.

Johnston, Hank, and Carol Mueller. 2001. "Unobtrusive Practices of Contention in Leninist Regimes." *Sociological Perspectives* 44: 351–76.

Johnston, Hank, and Seraphim Seferiades. 2012. "The Greek December." pp. 149–59 in *Violent Protest, Contentious Politics, and the Neoliberal State*," edited by Hank Johnston and Seraphim Seferiades. Farnham: Ashgate.

Juris, Jeffery S. 2005. "The New Digital Media and Activist Networking within the Anti-Corporate Globalization Movements." *Annals of the American Academy of Political and Social Sciences* 597: 189–208.

Kitschelt, Herbert. 1985. "New Social Movements in West Germany and the United States." *Political Power and Social Theory* 5: 273–342.

Kitschelt, Herbert. 1986. "Political Opportunity Structures and Political Protest: Anti-Nuclear Movements in Four Democracies." *British Journal of Political Science* 16: 57–85.

Klandermans, Bert, and Dirk Oegema. 1987. "Potentials, Networks, Motivations, Barriers: Steps toward Participation in Social Movements." *American Sociological Review* 52: 519–31.

Klandermans, Bert, and Jackie Smith. 2002. "Survey Research: A Case for Comparative Designs." pp. 3–31 in *Methods of Social Movement Research*, edited by Bert Klandermans and Susan Staggenborg. Minneapolis: University of Minnesota Press.

Klapp, Orin. 1969. *Collective Search for Identity*. New York: Holt, Rinehart, and Winston.

Kniss, Fred, and Gene Burns. 2004. "Religious Movements." pp. 694–715 in *The Blackwell Companion to Social Movements*, edited by David A. Snow, Sarah A. Soule, and Hanspeter Kriesi. Malden, MA: Blackwell.

Knoke, David. 1986. "Associations and Interest Groups." *Annual Review of Sociology* 12: 1–21.

Koopmans, Ruud, and Hanspeter Kriesi. 1995. "Institutional Structures and Prevailing Strategies." pp. 26–52 in *New Social Movements in Western Europe*, edited by Hanspeter Kriesi, Ruud Koopmans, Jan Willem Duyvendak, and Marco Giugni. Minneapolis: University of Minnesota Press.

Koopmans, Ruud, and Dieter Rucht. 2002. "Protest Event Analysis." pp. 231–59 in *Methods of Social Movement Research*, edited by Bert Klandermans and Susan Staggenborg. Minneapolis: University of Minnesota Press.

Koopmans, Ruud, and Paul Statham. 1999. "Political Claims Analysis: Integrating Protest Event and Public Discourse Approaches." *Mobilization: An International Quarterly* 4: 203–22.

Kornhauser, William. 1959. *The Politics of Mass Society.* Glencoe, IL: The Free Press.

Kousis, Maria, 1999. "Environmental Protest Cases: The City, The Countryside, and the Grassroots." *Mobilization: An International Quarterly* 4: 223–38.

Kriemer, Seth F. 2001. "Technologies of Protest: Insurgent Social Movements and the First Amendment in the Era of the Internet." *University of Pennsylvania Law Review* 150: 119–71.

Kriesi, Hanspeter. 1989. "New Social Movements and the New Class in the Netherlands." *American Journal of Sociology* 94: 1078–116.

Kriesi, Hanspeter. 1995. "The Political Opportunity Structure of New Social Movements: Its Impact on Their Mobilization." pp. 167–98 in *The Politics of Social Protest*, edited by J. Craig Jenkins and Bert Klandermans. Minneapolis: University of Minnesota Press.

Kriesi, Hanspeter, Ruud Koopmans, Jan Willem Duyvendak, and Marco Giugni. 1995. *New Social Movements in Western Europe: A Comparative Analysis.* Minneapolis: University of Minnesota Press.

Kuran, Timur. 1995. *Private Lives, Public Truths.* Cambridge, MA: Harvard University Press.

Kuumba, M. Bahati, and Femi Ajanaku. 1998. "Dreadlocks: The Hair Asesthetics of Cultural Resistance and Collective Identity Formation." *Mobilization: An International Quarterly* 3: 227–44.

Kwon, Roy, Ellen Reese, and Kadambari Anantran. 2008. "Core–Periphery Divisions Among Labor Activists at the World Social Forum." *Mobilization: An International Quarterly* 13: 411–30.

Lahusen, Christian. 2005. "Joining the Cocktail Circuit: Social Movement Organizations at the European Union." *Mobilization: An International Quarterly* 9: 55–72.

Latour, Bruno. 1987. *Science in Action.* Philadelphia: Open University Press.

Lavrakas, Paul J. 2008. *Encyclopedia of Survey Research Methods.* Thousand Oaks, CA: Sage.

Leach, Darcy, and Sebastian Haunss. 2009. "Scenes and Social Movements." pp. 255–76 in *Culture, Social Movements, and Protest*, edited by Hank Johnston. Farnham: Ashgate.

Le Bon, Gustave. 1960 [1894]. *The Crowd: A Study of the Popular Mind.* New York: Viking.

Lévi-Strauss, Claude. 1963. *Structural Anthropology.* Garden City, NY: Doubleday.

Lichbach, Mark I. 1997. "Contentous Maps of Contentious Politics." *Mobilization* 2: 87–98.

Lichterman, Paul. 2002. "Seeing Structure Happen: Theory-Driven Participant Observation." pp. 118–45 in *Methods of Social Movement Research*, edited by Bert Klandermans and Susan Staggenborg. Minneapolis: University of Minnesota Press.

Li-Sun, Joseph Yun. 2009. "Pyongyang: People Protest against the Poverty Generated by the New Currency." *Asia News*, accessed Feb. 15, 2010, www.asianews.it/index. php?I=en&art=17068& size=.

Maeckelbergh, Marianne. 2011. "The Road to Democracy: The Political Legacy of 1968." *International Review of Social History* 56: 301–32.

Maney, Gregory M., Rachel V. Flamenbaum, Deana A. Rohlinger, and Jeff Goodwin. 2012. *Strategies for Social Change*. Minneapolis: University of Minnesota Press.

Mannheim, Karl, 1940. *Man and Society in an Age of Reconstruction*. London: Kegan Paul.

McAdam, Doug. 1988. *Freedom Summer*. New York: Oxford University Press.

McAdam, Doug. 1999 [1982]. *Political Process and the Development of Black Insurgency, 1930–1970*. Second edition. Chicago: University of Chicago Press.

McAdam, Doug, and Dieter Rucht. 1993. "Cross-National Diffusion of Movement Ideas: The American 'New Left' and the European New Social Movements." *The Annals of the American Academy of Political and Social Sciences* 528: 56–74.

McAdam, Doug, and Sidney Tarrow. 2011. "Dynamics of Contention Ten Years On." *Mobilization* 16: 1–10.

McAdam, Doug, and Yang Su. 2002. "The War at Home: Anti-War Protests and Congressional Voting, 1965–73." *American Sociological Review* 67: 696–721.

McAdam Doug, John D. McCarthy, and Mayer N. Zald. 1996. "Introduction: Opportunities, Mobilizing Structures, and Framing Processes – Toward a Synthetic, Comparative Perspective on Social Movements." pp. 1–20 in *Comparative Perspectives on Social Movements: Political Opportunities, Mobilizing Structures, and Cultural Framings*, edited by Doug McAdam, John D. McCarthy, and Mayer N. Zald. New York: Cambridge University Press.

McAdam, Doug, Sidney Tarrow, and Charles Tilly. 2001. *The Dynamics of Contention*. New York: Cambridge University Press.

McCarthy, John D., and Mayer N. Zald. 1973. *The Trend of Social Movements in America: Professionalization and Resource Mobilization*. Morristown, NJ: General Learning Press.

McCarthy, John D., and Mayer N. Zald. 1977. "Resource Mobilization and Social Movements: A Partial Theory." *American Journal of Sociology* 82: 1212–41.

McCarthy, John D., Clark McPhail, and Jackie Smith. 1996. "Images of Protest: Dimensions of Selection Bias in Media Coverage of Washington Demonstrations, 1982–1991." *American Sociological Review* 61: 478–99.

McNeill, David. 2009. "North Koreans Dare to Protest as Devaluation Wipes Out Savings." *The Independent*, December 3.

McPhail, Clark. 1971. "Civil Disorder and Participation: A Critical Examination of Recent Research." *American Sociological Review* 36: 1058.

Melucci, Alberto. 1980. "The New Social Movements: A Theoretical Approach." *Social Science Information* 19.

Melucci, Alberto, ed. 1984. *Altri Codici: Aree di movimento nella metropoli*. Bologna: Il Mulino.

Melucci, Alberto. 1985. "The Symbolic Challenge of Contemporary Movements." *Social Research* 52: 789–816.

Melucci, Alberto. 1989. *Nomads of the Present: Social Movements and Individual Needs in Contemporary Society*. Philadelphia: Temple University Press.

Melucci, Alberto. 1996. *Challenging Codes*. New York: Cambridge University Press.

Meyer, David S., and Nella Van Dyke. 2014. *Understanding the Tea Party Movement*. Farnham: Ashgate.

Meyer, David S., and Suzanne Staggenborg. 1996. "Movements, Countermovements and the Structure of Political Opportunity." *American Journal of Sociology* 101: 628–60.

Meyer, David S., and Sidney Tarrow. 1998. *Social Movement Society*. Lanham, MD: Rowman & Littlefield.

Meyer, David S., and Nancy Whittier. 1994. "Social Movement Spillover." *Social Problems* 41: 277–98.

Michels, Robert. 1962 [1911]. *Political Parties: A Sociological Study of the Oligarchical Tendencies of Modern Democracy*. New York: Free Press.

Minkoff, Debra C. 1994. "From Service Provision to Institutional Advocacy: The Shifting Legitimacy of Organizational Forms." *Social Forces* 72: 943–69.

Minkoff, Debra C. 1995. *Organizing for Equality: The Evolution of Women's Racial Ethnic Organizations in America, 1955–1985*. New Brunswick, NJ: Rutgers University Press.

Minkoff, Debra. 1997. "The Sequencing of Social Movements." *American Sociological Review* 62: 779–99.

Minkoff, Debra, and David Meyer. 2004. "Conceptualizing Political Opportunity." *Social Forces* 82: 1457–92.

Mische, Ann. 2003. "Cross-Talk in Movements: Reconceiving the Culture–Network Link." pp. 258–80 in *Social Movements and Networks*, edited by Mario Diani and Doug McAdam. New York: Oxford University Press.

Moore, Ryan, and Michael Roberts. 2009. "Do-It-Yourself Mobilization: Punk and Social Movements." *Mobilization: An International Quarterly* 14: 273–92.

Morris, Aldon. 1984. *The Origins of the Civil Rights Movement: Black Communities Organizing for Change.* New York: The Free Press.

Mueller, Carol. 1997. "Media Measurement Models of Protest Event Data." *Mobilization: An International Quarterly* 2: 165–84.

Murphy, Kim. 2012. "Greenpeace Forced to Get More Creative." *Los Angeles Times*, June 10: A15.

Myers, Daniel J. 1994. "Communication Technology and Social Movements: Contributions of Computer Networks to Activism." *Social Science Computer Review* 12: 250–60.

Myers, Daniel J. 1997. "Racial Rioting in the 1960s: An Event History Analysis of Local Conditions." *American Sociological Review* 62: 94–112.

Myers, Daniel J. 2010. "Violent Protest and Heterogeneous Diffusion Processes: The Spread of U.S. Racial Rioting, 1964–1971." *Mobilization: An International Quarterly* 15: 289–322.

Norton, Ann. 2004. *Ninety-Five Theses on Politics, Culture, and Method.* New Haven, CT: Yale University Press.

Oberschall, Anthony. 1968. "Rising Expectations and Political Turmoil." *Journal of Development Studies* 6: 5–22.

Oberschall, Anthony. 1973. *Social Conflict and Social Movements.* Englewood Cliffs, NJ: Prentice Hall.

Olesen, Thomas. 2005. *International Zapatismo.* London: Zed Books.

Oliver, Pamela E., and Hank Johnston. 2005 "What a Good Idea: Frames and Ideology in Social Movement Theory." pp. 185–203 in *Frames of Protest*, edited by Hank Johnston and John Noakes. Lanham, MD: Rowman and Littlefield Publishers.

Oliver, Pamela E., and Daniel J. Myers. 1999. "How Events Enter the Public Sphere." *American Journal of Sociology* 106: 38–87.

Olson, Mancur. 1963. *The Logic of Collective Action.* Cambridge, MA: Harvard University Press.

Olzak, Susan, Maya Beasley, and Johan Olivier. 2003. "The Impact of State Reforms on Protest Against Apartheid in South Africa." *Mobilization: An International Quarterly* 8: 27–50.

Ortega y Gasset, José. 1932. *Revolt of the Masses*. New York: W. W. Norton.

Oselin, Sharon S., and Catherine Corrigall-Brown. 2010. "A Battle for Authenticity: An Examination of the Constraints on Anti-Iraq and Pro-Invasion Tactics." *Mobilization: An International Quarterly* 15: 511–33.

Oslzly, Petr. 1990. "On Stage with the Velvet Revolution." *Drama Review* 34(3): 88–96.

Pareles, Jon. 2007. "Rock 'n' Revolution." *New York Times*, November 11, AR: 1–32.

Park, Robert, and Ernest Burgess. 1969 [1921]. *An Introduction to the Science of Sociology*. Chicago: University of Chicago Press.

Pfaff, Steven. 1996. "Collective Identity and Informal Groups in Revolutionary Mobilization: East Germany in 1989." *Social Forces* 75: 91–118.

Piven, Frances Fox. 2012. "Protest Movements and Violence." pp. 19–28 in *Violent Protest, Contentious Politics, and the Neo-liberal State*, edited by Seraphim Seferiades and Hank Johnston. Farnham: Ashgate.

Piven, Frances Fox, and Richard Cloward. 1977. *Poor People's Movements*. New York: Pantheon.

Pleyers, Geoffrey. 2011. *Alterglobalization: Becoming Actors in the Global Age*. Malden, MA: Blackwell.

Polletta, Francesca. 2002. *Freedom is an Endless Meeting: Democracy in American Social Movements*. Chicago: University of Chicago Press.

Polletta, Francesca. 2006a. *It Was Like a Fever: Storytelling in Protest and Politics*. Chicago: University of Chicago Press.

Polletta, Francesca. 2006b. "Mobilization Forum: Awkward Movements." *Mobilization: An International Quarterly* 11: 475–78.

Polletta, Francesca. 2009. "Storytelling in Social Movements." pp. 33–53 in *Culture, Social Movements and Protest*, edited by Hank Johnston. Farnham: Ashgate.

Ramos, Howard. 2008. "Opportunity for Whom? Political Opportunity and Critical Events in Canadian Aboriginal Mobilization 1951–2000." *Social Forces* 87: 795–823.

Raney, Rebecca Fairley. 1999. "Flash Campaigns: Online Activism at Warp Speed." *New York Times*, June 3. Accessed June 6, 2012. www.nytimes.com/library/tech/99/06/cyber/articles/03campaign.html.

Rochon, Thomas R. 1998. *Culture Moves: Ideas, Activism, and Changing Values.* Princeton, NJ: Princeton University Press.

Romero, Simon. 2013a. "Thousands Gather for Protests in Brazil's Largest Cities." *New York Times,* June 18: A5.

Romero, Simon. 2013b. "Protests Widen as Brazilians Chide Leaders." *New York Times,* June 19: A1.

Rosenthal, Bob, and Richard Flacks. 2012. *Playing for Change: Music and Musicians in the Service of Social Movements.* Boulder, CO: Paradigm Publishers.

Rosigno, Vincent J., and William F. Danaher. 2004. *The Voice of Southern Labor.* Minneapolis: University of Minnesota Press.

Rucht, Dieter. 1996. "The Impact of National Contexts on Social Movements Structure." pp. 185–204 in *Comparative Perspectives on Social Movements: Political Opportunities, Mobilizing Structures, and Cultural Framings,* edited by Doug McAdam, John D. McCarthy, and Mayer N. Zald. New York: Cambridge University Press.

Rucht, Dieter. 1998. "The Structure and Culture of Collective Protest in Germany since 1950." pp. 29–57 in *The Social Movement Society: Contentious Politics for a New Century,* edited by David Meyer and Sidney Tarrow. Boulder, CO: Rowman & Littlefield.

Rucht, Dieter, Ruud Koopmans, and Friedhelm Neidhardt, eds. 1999. *Acts of Dissent: New Developments in the Study of Protest.* Lanham, MD: Rowman and Littlefield.

Runciman, W. G. 1966. *Relative Deprivation and Social Justice.* London: Routledge, Kegan Paul.

Rupp, Leila, and Verta Taylor. 2003. *Drag Queens at the 801 Cabernet.* Chicago: University of Chicago Press.

Ryan, Charlotte. 1991. *Prime Time Activism.* Boston: South End.

Schmidt, Michael S. 2012. "For Occupy Movement, A Challenge to Recapture Momentum." *New York Times,* April 1: A19.

Schrodt, Phillip A. 2006. "Twenty Years of the Kansas Event Data System Project," accessed January 17, 2012, www.ku.edu/_keds/KEDS.history.html.

Selbin, Eric. 2010. *Revolution, Rebellion, and Resistance: The Power of Story.* London: Zed Books.

Shefner, Jon, George Pasdirtz, and Cory Blad. 2006. "Austerity Protests and Immiserating Growth in Mexico and Argentina." pp. 19–42 in *Latin American Social Movements,* edited by Hank Johnston and Paul Almeida. Lanham, MD: Rowman and Littlefield.

Shultziner, Doron. 2013. "The Social-Psychological Origins of the Montgomery Bus Boycott: Social Interaction and Humiliation in the Emergence of Social Movements." *Mobilization: An International Quarterly* 18: 117–38.

Simon, Herbert W. 1990. *The Rhetorical Turn: Invention and Persuasion in the Conduct of Inquiry.* Chicago: University of Chicago Press.

Smith, Jackie. 2002. "Globalizing Resistance: The Battle of Seattle and the Future of Social Movements." pp. 207–26 in *Globalization and Resistance: Transnational Dimensions of Social Movements*, edited by Jackie Smith and Hank Johnston. Lanham, MD: Rowman & Littlefield.

Smith, Jackie. 2008. *Social Movements for Global Democracy.* Baltimore, MD: Johns Hopkins University Press.

Smith, Jackie, and Ellen Reese. 2008. "The World Social Forum Process: Special Focus Issue." *Mobilization: An International Quarterly* 13: 349–446.

Snow, David A., and Robert D. Benford. 1988. "Ideology, Frame Resonance, and Participant Mobilization." pp. 197–217 in *International Social Movement Research*, edited by Bert Klandermans, Hanspeter Kriesi, and Sidney Tarrow. Greenwich, CT: JAI Press.

Snow, David A., and Robert D. Benford. 1992. "Master Frames and Cycles of Protest." pp. 133–55 in *Frontiers of Social Movement Theory*, edited by Aldon Morris and Carol McClurg Mueller. New Haven, CT: Yale University Press.

Snow, David A., and Robert D. Benford. 1999. "Alternative Types of Crossnational Diffusion in the Social Movements Arena." pp. 23–39 in *Social Movements in a Globalizing World*, edited by Donatella della Porta, Hanspeter Kriesi, and Dieter Rucht. London: Macmillan.

Snow, David A., Robert D. Benford, Holly J. McCammon, Lyndi Hewitt, and Scott Fitzgerald. 2013. "The Emergence of the Framing Perspective: What Lies Ahead?" *Mobilization* 18: 457–75.

Snow, David A., Hank Johnston, and Garth McCallum. 1994. "Subcultures of Resistance and Collective Action." A paper presented at Session on Sociology of Culture, Pacific Sociological Association Annual Meetings, April 14–17, San Diego, CA.

Snow, David A., E. Burke Rochford, Jr., Steven K. Worden, and Robert D. Benford. 1986. "Frame Alignment Processes, Micromobilization, and Movement Participation." *American Sociological Review* 51: 464–81.

Snow, David A., Robert D. Benford, Holly J. McCammon, Lyndi Hewitt, and Scott Fitzgerald. 2014. "The Emergence of the

Framing Perspective: What Lies Ahead?" *Mobilization* 19: 1–24.

Soule, Sarah A. 1997. "The Student Divestment Movement in the United States and Tactical Diffusion: Shantytown Protests." *Social Forces* 71: 431–49.

Soule, Sarah A., and Jennifer Earl. 2005. "A Movement Society Revisited: The Character of American Social Protest, 1960–1986." *Mobilization: An International Quarterly* 10: 345–64.

Steinberg, Marc. 1999. *Fighting Words*. Ithaca, NY: Cornell University Press.

Swidler, Ann. 1995. "Cultural Power and Social Movements." pp. 25–40 in *Social Movements and Culture*, edited by Hank Johnston and Bert Klandermans. Minneapolis: Univeristy of Minnesota Press.

Tarrow, Sidney. 1983. *Struggling to Reform: Social Movements and Policy Change During Cycles of Protest. Western Societies Paper 15*. Ithaca, NY: Cornell University.

Tarrow, Sidney. 1989. *Democracy and Disorder: Protest and Politics in Italy, 1965–1975*. Oxford: Clarendon.

Tarrow, Sidney. 1998. *Power in Movement*. New York: Cambridge University Press.

Tarrow, Sidney. 2005. *The New Transnational Activism*. New York: Cambridge University Press.

Taylor, Verta, and Nicole C. Raeburn. 1995. "Identity Politics as High-Risk Activism: Career Consequences for Lesbian, Gay, and Bisexual Sociologists." *Social Problems* 42: 252–73.

Taylor, Verta, and Nancy E. Whittier. 1992. "Collective Identity in Social Movement Communities." pp. 104–29 in *Frontiers in Social Movement Theory*, edited by Aldon Morris and Carol McClurg Mueller. New Haven, CT: Yale University Press.

Thrall, T. A. 2006. "The Myth of the Outside Strategy: Mass Media News Coverage of Interest Groups." *Political Communication* 23: 407–20.

Tilly, Charles. 1978. *From Mobilization to Revolution*. Reading, MA: Addison-Wesley.

Tilly, Charles. 1986. *The Contentious French*. Cambridge, MA: Harvard University Press.

Tilly, Charles. 1995. *Popular Contention in Great Britain 1758–1834*. Cambridge, MA: Harvard University Press.

Tilly, Charles. 2006. *Regimes and Repertoires*. Chicago: University of Chicago Press.

Tilly, Charles. 2007. *Democracy*. New York: Cambridge University Press.

Tilly, Charles, 2008. *Contentious Performances*. New York: Cambridge University Press.

Tilly, Charles, and Lesley J. Wood. 2009. *Social Movements, 1768–2008*. Boulder, CO: Paradigm Publishers.

Turner, Ralph. 1969. "The Theme of Contemporary Social Movements." *British Journal of Sociology* 20: 390–405.

Turner, Ralph. 1996. "The Moral Issue in Collective Action." *Mobilization: An International Quarterly* 1: 1–15.

Turner, Ralph, and Lewis Killian. 1987 [1957]. *Collective Behavior*. Englewood Cliffs, NJ: Prentice Hall.

Vala, Carsten T., and Kevin J. O'Brien. 2007. "Attraction without Networks: Recruiting Strangers to Unregistered Protestantism in China." *Mobilization: An International Quarterly* 12: 79–94.

Van Dyke, Nella, and Sarah A. Soule. 2002. "Structural Social Change and the Mobilizing Effect of Threat: Explaining Levels of Patriot and Militia Mobilizing in the United States, 1930–1990." *Social Problems* 49: 497–520.

Von Bülow, Marisa. 2011. "Brokers in Action: Transnational Coalitions and Trade Agreements in the Americas." *Mobilization: An International Quarterly* 16: 164–80.

Walker, Jack L. 1991. *Mobilizing Interest Groups in America: Patrons, Professions, and Social Movements*. Ann Arbor: University of Michigan Press.

Wellman, Barry. 2001. "Physical Place and Cyberspace." *International Journal of Urban and Regional Research* 25: 227–52.

White, Robert W. 1999. "Comparing State Repression of Pro-State Vigilantes and Anti-State Insurgents: Northern Ireland 1972–1975." *Mobilization: An International Quarterly* 4: 203–22.

Whittier, Nancy. 1995. *Feminist Generations*. Philadelphia: Temple University Press.

Wilson, Christopher, and Alexandra Dunn. 2011. "Digital Media in the Egyptian Revolution: Descriptive Analysis from the Tahrir Data Set." *International Journal of Communication* 5: 1248–72.

Wolsfeld, Gadi. 1997. *Media and Political Conflict: News from the Middle East*. New York: Cambridge University Press.

Wuthnow, Robert. 1989. *Communities of Discourse*. Cambridge, MA: Harvard University Press.

Young, Michael. 2002. "Confessional Protest: The Religious Birth of U.S. National Social Movements." *American Sociological Review* 67: 660–88.

Zald, Mayer N. 2010. "Career, Collaborations, and a Next Step: Profiles of Institutional Collective Action Potentials." *Mobilization: An International Quarterly* 15: 249–66.

Zald, Mayer N., and Roberta Ash. 1966. "Social Movement Organizations: Growth, Decay, and Change." *Social Forces* 44: 327–40.

Zald, Mayer N., and John D. McCarthy. 1987. "Social Movement Industries: Competition and Conflicts among SMOs." pp. 161–84 in *Social Movements in an Organizational Society: Collective Essays*, edited by Mayer N. Zald and John D. McCarthy. New Brunswick, NJ: Transaction.

Index